TO BE FOUND IN CHRIST

A STUDY IN PHILIPPIANS

CHRISTIAN SARMIENTO

BEACON HILL PRESS
OF KANSAS CITY

Copyright © 2016 by Christian Sarmiento
Beacon Hill Press of Kansas City
PO Box 419527
Kansas City, MO 64141
beaconhillbooks.com

978-0-8341-3603-8

Printed in the
United States of America

Cover Design: Merit Alcala
Interior Design: Sharon Page

Library of Congress Cataloging-in-Publication Data
Names: Sarmiento, Christian, 1956- author.
Title: To be found in Christ / Christian Sarmiento.
Description: Kansas City, MO : Beacon Hill Press, 2016.
Identifiers: LCCN 2016024747 | ISBN 9780834136038 (pbk.)
Subjects: LCSH: Bible. Philippians—Devotional literature. | Christian life—
Biblical teaching.
Classification: LCC BS2705.54 .S37 2016 | DDC 227/.606—dc23 LC record available at
https://lccn.loc.gov/2016024747

10 9 8 7 6 5 4 3 2 1

To my beloved wife, Margit,
who read each devotional daily, corrected it,
made suggestions, and sent it to others.
Thank you!

CONTENTS

Unit 2: The Mind of Christ, the Model for Christians

Unit 3: Dangers in the Church

Unit 4: Healthy Counsel

Foreword

To enter into the study of the letter from the apostle Paul to the Philippians is to open a window to the heart and thought of the author regarding the victorious Christian life despite difficult circumstances. Paul is found in Christ, even though this means that he writes from prison for the cause of Christ. I encourage you to follow Dr. Sarmiento's methodology to extract the advice given by the apostle Paul to grow in your faith in Christ, to understand the purposes of God, and to know what goals and values cannot be negotiated under any circumstance.

To Be Found in Christ will lead us to the place God has reserved for each person in this life and in eternity. It is not only a physical place, but it is founded in the Word, the values, and the principles of the Lord. Dr. Sarmiento's reflections, using other books of the Bible and other letters from the same apostle, will not only strengthen you, making a difference in your life, but will also encourage you to develop the fruit of love in the power of the Holy Spirit. This love will then become the oil in your relationships with others.

For Paul, the life of Jesus Christ is always the example to follow to look inside ourselves and imitate him. Paul does this in his own life and desires to reproduce Christ in his readers—the brothers and sisters in the churches of Asia Minor. He loves them so much that he wants to transmit the message with the greatest faithfulness possible.

To Be Found in Christ helps us discover the message for today: A life of holiness is not just an ideal; it is the kind of life God has designed for us here on earth, preparing us for eternity. Leaning on the examples of Christ and Paul, discover yourself as a Christian, a servant leader, part of a team, and part of a church where Christ is the head. We are members of Christ's body, fulfilling the function with which he has entrusted us.

To Be Found in Christ is a complete challenge for the disciples of Christ, not for a day or a short time. It is the reason for being from before the foundation of the world. This is when God sent his Son, Jesus Christ, who voluntarily decided to die on the cross for our sins. He rose again and then sent the Holy Spirit to be with us every day until the end of the world.

Dr. Carlos Hugo Fernández
Retired Missionary

UNIT 1
AN OLD MAN, A YOUNG MAN, AND ORDINARY PEOPLE

1

PAUL AND TIMOTHY

SCRIPTURE
Philippians 1:1

DEVOTIONAL REFLECTION

A letter is always welcome if it is from a loved one, even when technology has changed many customs. We will always be glad to receive news from someone we love. However, many times the circumstances are not as good for those who write.

Paul and Timothy are two people in different stages of life; one of them is trying to transmit his experience and passion for preaching the gospel, and the other one is preparing, with a willing heart, to continue with his calling.

Paul is a prisoner in Rome, and along with Timothy, they greet the church by introducing themselves as "servants" (by which he likely means "slaves"). Paul has been bought by Jesus Christ to be set free. Voluntarily and because of love, Paul has decided that Jesus will be his owner and his Lord. He is willing to go to the ends of the earth to serve him, spreading his love to thousands and thousands of people.

The older man is accompanied by a young man, Timothy, whom Paul disciples and will soon send to Philippi to strengthen and encourage the church in that city. A servant (or slave) of Christ obeys the Great Commission to "make disciples of all nations." Only a person who has surrendered the lordship of self can be a disciple of Jesus. That person then becomes the slave of Jesus and serves him faithfully, knowing that Jesus is the most loving Master in the world.

Something to bear in mind is that in ancient times, when a Hebrew servant is bought, he has to be set free after seven years, unless the servant chooses to remain with his master. At that point, he freely chooses to be a lifelong servant.

The book of Philippians will help us appreciate the great love of God and lead us to a commitment to surrender completely to God. Remember, in each prayer you offer, to give thanks for the freedom from sin that God, through Jesus Christ, has provided us with the blood of Jesus shed on the cross.

Do the leaders of your church have young disciples who are involved in ministry? Are you serving in any way as a response to the freedom Christ has given you?

SCRIPTURAL CONTEXT

But if the servant declares, "I love my master and my wife and children and do not want to go free," then his master must take him before the judges. He shall take him to the door or the doorpost and pierce his ear with an awl. Then he will be his servant for life. (Exodus 21:5–6)

And whoever wants to be first must be your slave—just as the Son of Man did not come to be served, but to serve, and to give his life as a ransom for many. (Matthew 20:27–28)

For you know that it was not with perishable things such as silver or gold that you were redeemed from the empty way of life . . . but with the precious blood of Christ, a lamb without blemish or defect. (1 Peter 1:18–19)

JOURNAL

Make a list of people you can commit to pray for and disciple as Christ followers.

_____

_____

_____

_____

_____

_____

_____

_____

_____

_____

_____

_____

_____

_____

_____

_____

_____

_____

_____

_____

_____

_____

_____

_____

_____

_____

_____

_____

_____

_____

PRAYER

Lord, thank you for the disciples who accompany us in our ministry.
Ask what you want from us; we are your servants.

2
HOLY PEOPLE?

SCRIPTURE
Philippians 1:1

DEVOTIONAL REFLECTION

The church is strengthened if it has people who are willing to work as a team, seeking to advance the kingdom of God in every area. Timothy is a young man, and Paul is an elder. Together they are devoted to one task—that of writing "to all God's holy people." Paul is sure that, in the church in Philippi, there are holy people.

The word *holy* appears 454 times in both the Old and New Testaments. Holiness and redemption are God's goal for all of humanity. The key to holiness is in the phrase that Paul uses: "in Christ Jesus." We can only be holy *in* Christ. He saves us and cleanses us. He makes us holy. He transforms our being. He transforms our fallen nature. We cannot be holy on our own.

Jesus Christ not only sanctifies us, giving us the quality of being holy people, but he also separates us to be used in mission. Jesus prays in John 17:17–18: "Sanctify them by the truth; your word is truth. As you sent me into the world, I have sent them into the world." God expects us to be holy.

Holiness is not for people of the past who lived righteously and who are now venerated. Holiness is for people who live today in a world filled with darkness, corruption, selfishness, and evil. Holiness is for the whole world and those who believe. God sends us to the world to shine in any environment, circumstance, and culture.

As holy ones in Christ Jesus, we can claim with Paul: "No, in all these things we are more than conquerors through him who loved us" (Romans 8:37).

Scriptural Context

I am the LORD your God; consecrate yourselves and be holy, because I am holy. . . . I am the LORD, who brought you up out of Egypt to be your God; therefore be holy, because I am holy. (Leviticus 11:44a–45).

To all in Rome who are loved by God and called to be his holy people: Grace and peace to you from God our Father and from the Lord Jesus Christ. (Romans 1:7)

For Further Study
Leviticus 19:1–2
Leviticus 20:7
Matthew 27:52
Acts 9:13
2 Corinthians 13:13–14

Journal

Explain what you think the expression *holy people* means. Study the passages listed above. Then, briefly write what it means to be holy people of God.

_____

_____

_____

_____

_____

_____

_____

_____

_____

_____

_____

_____

_____

_____

_____

_____

_____

_____

_____

_____

_____

_____

_____

_____

_____

_____

_____

_____

_____

_____

_____

_____

_____

PRAYER

Lord, help us depend on you and to live *in* you. We ask for forgiveness for trying to live in holiness on our own strength, relying on our own abilities, personalities, and character traits. We know you are the One who does "immeasurably more than all we ask or imagine, according to [your] power that is at work within us" (Ephesians 3:20).

3

MINISTERING WITH OUR AUTHORITIES

SCRIPTURE
Philippians 1:1

DEVOTIONAL REFLECTION
Notice the interesting progression of Paul's greeting: (a) "to all God's holy people;" (b) "in Christ Jesus;" (c) "at Philippi;" (d) "together with the overseers and deacons." We could read this verse in the following way: (a) a holy church; (b) centered in Christ; (c) that ministers in its community; (d) that has leaders to train the holy ones for the work of the ministry.

The phrase "together with the overseers and deacons" is interesting. It doesn't say that the overseers and the deacons are the bosses of the holy people in Philippi. It says they work *together*. Without a doubt, this greeting discards completely any kind of authoritarian leadership guided by selfishness or competition. It shows a type of leadership that implies a relationship of love and tolerance.

The overseer is attentive to the spirituality, the conduct, the learning process, and the strategy of the church for it to grow. The goal is a holistic Christian community that grows, where all the holy people are involved in ministry *together* with their leaders.

The Father, Son, and Holy Spirit designate church leaders. God calls some to be overseers, others to be deacons (servants), others to be teachers, others to be pastors, and still others to be missionaries. Everyone in the body of Christ has a calling and a ministry. It is good to know that the organization of the church has been instituted by God to guide it to be efficient, productive, and to fill the earth with his glory!

May God help you find your place in the body of Christ and, above all, for Christ to be the head that directs and encourages you to go forward. Let us allow those whom God has called to each office fulfill their tasks and ministries. Let us be bridges for their growth and not stumbling blocks. Always remember that God will ask us for an accounting of each person he has placed in our circle of ministry.

SCRIPTURAL CONTEXT

Keep watch over yourselves and all the flock of which the Holy Spirit has made you overseers. Be shepherds of the church of God, which he bought with his own blood. (Acts 20:28)

Let everyone be subject to the governing authorities, for there is no authority except that which God has established. The authorities that exist have been established by God. Consequently, whoever rebels against the authority is rebelling against what God has instituted, and those who do so will bring judgment on themselves. For rulers hold no terror for those who do right, but for those who do wrong. Do you want to be free from fear of the one in authority? Then do what is right and you will be commended. (Romans 13:1–3)

Remember your leaders, who spoke the word of God to you. Consider the outcome of their way of life and imitate their faith. (Hebrews 13:7)

Have confidence in your leaders and submit to their authority, because they keep watch over you as those who must give an account. Do this so that their work will be a joy, not a burden, for that would be of no benefit to you. (Hebrews 13:17)

For Further Study
Acts 6:3–6
Ephesians 4:11–12
Titus 3:1

JOURNAL

If you are a leader in your church, what type of leadership do you live out? Write the names of the leaders of your church, and pray for them.

_____

_____

_____

_____

_____

_____

_____

_____

_____

_____

_____

_____

_____

_____

_____

_____

_____

_____

_____

_____

_____

_____

PRAYER

Thank you, Lord, for establishing leaders in our church. Help us love them, respect them, and listen to their loving advice. Protect them from evil and temptation.

4
GRACE AND PEACE

SCRIPTURE
Philippians 1:2

DEVOTIONAL REFLECTION
Paul's greeting is a blessing for the church in Philippi. The first thing Paul does in the letter is bless his brothers and sisters in Christ. We can really only bless others with something we ourselves have received. Paul wants to bless them with the most precious thing he has received—grace and peace.

Grace and peace are treasures Paul has received "from God our Father and the Lord Jesus Christ." The quality of the gift is measured by the quality of the giver. It is incredible to know that grace and peace come from God our Father, through the sacrifice of the Lord Jesus Christ, because of the presence of the Holy Spirit in our lives.

If we have received grace and peace ourselves, then it is the best blessing we can offer others. Let us ask for grace and peace from God our Father and the Lord Jesus Christ in every personal relationship, in every circumstance, for everyone we know, and for those whom God will place in our pathways.

SCRIPTURAL CONTEXT
The LORD bless you and keep you; the LORD make his face shine on you and be gracious to you; the LORD turn his face toward you and give you peace. (Numbers 6:24–26)

If you then, though you are evil, know how to give good gifts to your children, how much more will your Father in heaven give the Holy Spirit to those who ask him! (Luke 11:13)

Praise be to the God and Father of our Lord Jesus Christ! In his great mercy he has given us new birth into a living hope through the resurrection of Jesus Christ from the dead, and into an inheritance that can never perish, spoil or fade. This inheritance is kept in heaven for you. (1 Peter 1:3–4)

JOURNAL

Maybe in this very moment God is bringing to your mind and heart the people who are close to you who need this gift. In what way can you communicate the blessing of grace and peace to them? Why is it important to ask the Lord for grace and peace? Consider the scriptures listed above in order to give your answer.

_____

_____

_____

_____

_____

_____

_____

_____

_____

_____

_____

_____

_____

_____

_____

PRAYER

Thank you, God, for blessing us with your grace and peace! Help us to bless others in the same way.

5 ❧
FOR FREE!

SCRIPTURE
Philippians 1:2

DEVOTIONAL REFLECTION

In the Greek secular world, "grace" is a favor bestowed by a king or dignitary upon another king or dignitary. It is an understanding between equals. Another favor (or "grace") is always expected in return. In the Old Testament, the equivalent word in Hebrew (*hen*) means mercy, piety, or clemency.

Grace is the gift of God through the death of Jesus Christ (see John 3:16) for everyone who wants to receive it. It is the gift of complete salvation, effected through the Holy Spirit—salvation from the sins we have committed, salvation from the source of sin, and continual salvation day by day, as long as we depend on the grace of God. God's action of saving us in Christ Jesus was performed between unequal entities. It was an act of God the Almighty, Creator, King of kings, Infinite, Majestic, Eternal, toward us—fallen people who are fallible, finite, and evil.

The grace of God is enough for each circumstance in life, not only to save us but also to sanctify us. Desiring the grace of God for others is blessing them. It is a prayer for complete protection and well-being. The grace of God is not extinct or scarce, but it also cannot be bought. It is free! God continues and continues to pour out grace. It is God's nature to bless us.

That is why it is important to pray for grace for others and for ourselves. Even though it is already available, this prayer is a reminder of the love, mercy, clemency, and piety of God toward all of us.

God continues to pour out his grace more and more! We need the Father to pour his abundant grace over us so we can, in turn, show it to those around us. Today we need the favor of God more than ever. We should ask God to help us be agents of his grace and love.

SCRIPTURAL CONTEXT

The Word became flesh and made his dwelling among us. We have seen his glory, the glory of the one and only Son, who came from the Father, full of grace and truth. (John 1:14)

Out of his fullness we have all received grace in place of grace already given. (John 1:16)

For all have sinned and fall short of the glory of God, and all are justified freely by his grace through the redemption that came by Christ Jesus. (Romans 3:23–24)

But he said to me, "My grace is sufficient for you, for my power is made perfect in weakness." Therefore I will boast all the more gladly about my weaknesses, so that Christ's power may rest on me. (2 Corinthians 12:9)

He has saved us and called us to a holy life—not because of anything we have done but because of his own purpose and grace. This grace was given us in Christ Jesus before the beginning of time. (2 Timothy 1:9)

For Further Study
Luke 1:28
1 Corinthians 1:4
Ephesians 1:5–6
1 Timothy 1:14–15
Hebrews 4:16
1 Peter 5:10–11

JOURNAL

Make a list of everything you have received from God in the past week. Thank God specifically for each one of his blessings. Write about a difficult situation of your life, and ask God for his grace to resolve it, and to be able to bear it while it is being resolved. Pray for God to bless those who have caused this situation in your life.

_____

_____

_____

_____

_____

_____

_____

_____

_____

_____

_____

_____

_____

_____

_____

_____

_____

_____

_____

_____

_____

_____

PRAYER

Father of all grace, give us your abundant grace today. Pour it over us so we can show it to those who surround us. Today we need, more than ever, more of your grace. Help us be agents of your grace and love.

6

COMPLETE HEALTH

SCRIPTURE
Philippians 1:2

DEVOTIONAL REFLECTION

The concept of the word *peace*, in the Old Testament (*shalom* and *eirene*), means complete health or an absence of contradiction. It is more than a state of tranquility or absence of war. Peace is unity of purpose. If my purpose is exactly the same as that of another person and we come to an agreement to fulfill it at any cost, we will have unity. That is to say, we will have peace. The Lord Jesus Christ prays in John 17 for us to be one with him and with the Father, resulting in the fruit of the Spirit of peace. The greeting-blessing that Paul offers to the Philippians is a desire for grace and peace.

Unfortunately, many times, we forget to give thanks for certain people, and we only have in mind the evil we think they do. Paul's desire for both grace *and* peace is the perfect combination—all of God's favor resulting in complete health. The state of complete health in God's favor is what each person desires; it is the internal search that gives us fullness.

It starts with a search for God. When we find God (or, rather, when God finds us), abide in God in obedience, and fix our eyes on God (see 2 Corinthians 3:18 and Hebrews 12:2), we live in peace and receive continually his transforming grace. What else can we ask for?

God is a God of peace. No other can offer the same peace. Jesus is the expression of the love of God and of his grace and peace (John 14:27). As we live in the Spirit, we receive the fruit of peace.

The kingdom of God is peace; to be filled with the Spirit is peace. Jesus is the agent of peace who represents the God of peace. Listening to God gives us peace, and in that way we will not return to our foolish ways (see Psalm 85:8).

SCRIPTURAL CONTEXT

I will listen to what God the LORD says; he promises peace to his people, his faithful servants—but let them not turn to folly. (Psalm 85:8)

Peace I leave with you; my peace I give you. I do not give to you as the world gives. Do not let your hearts be troubled and do not be afraid. (John 14:27)

You know the message God sent to the people of Israel, announcing the good news of peace through Jesus Christ, who is Lord of all. (Acts 10:36)

The mind governed by the flesh is death, but the mind governed by the Spirit is life and peace. (Romans 8:6)

For Further Study
Numbers 6:24–26
Job 25:2
Mark 5:34
John 20:19
Romans 14:17
1 Corinthians 14:33
Philippians 4:7

JOURNAL

Write the main purpose that you have for your life. Is that purpose within the will of God? How would that purpose need to change in order to be aligned with the will of God? Write the new version of your purpose once you have aligned it with the will of God.

_____

_____

_____

_____

_____

PRAYER

Now may the God of peace, who through the blood of the eternal covenant brought back from the dead our Lord Jesus, that great Shepherd of the sheep, equip you with everything good for doing his will, and may he work in us what is pleasing to him, through Jesus Christ, to whom be glory for ever and ever. Amen. (Hebrews 13:20–21)

7
I Will Pray for You

Scripture
Philippians 1:3

Devotional Reflection
Paul does not promise to pray for the Philippians at some arbitrary date in the future; rather, he rather affirms that he always remembers them in his prayers.

Giving thanks to God is a commandment of the Bible (see Ephesians 5:20). Giving thanks is an exercise of the will, both when we are doing well and when things are not going so well. Jesus models this practice for us, knowing that the Father is always listening to him (see John 11:41–42).

Let us begin to give thanks to God for everything. For the people we like and for those we do not. Each time someone or something comes to mind, let us thank God for that person or event. As we develop a mindset and habit of thanksgiving, we will grow closer to God and others. Let us get accustomed, like Paul, to pray constantly for others, whenever we think of them.

When we give thanks to God in difficult circumstances, it is a sign of faith that God is the one in control.

Scriptural Context
We praise you, God, we praise you, for your Name is near; people tell of your wonderful deeds. (Psalm 75:1)

Jesus then took the loaves, gave thanks, and distributed to those who were seated as much as they wanted. He did the same with the fish. (John 6:11)

So they took away the stone. Then Jesus looked up and said, "Father, I thank you that you have heard me. I knew that you always hear me, but I said this for the benefit of the people standing here, that they may believe that you sent me." (John 11:41–42)

But thanks be to God! He gives us the victory through our Lord Jesus Christ. (1 Corinthians 15:57)

Always giving thanks to God the Father for everything, in the name of our Lord Jesus Christ. (Ephesians 5:20)

JOURNAL

Make a prayer list for specific people who will be close to you this week, for the situations you will face, for your tasks, and for the work you have to do this week.

_____

_____

_____

_____

_____

_____

_____

_____

_____

_____

_____

PRAYER

Thank you, Lord, for your salvation, for my family, for your church, for my brothers and sisters in Christ, for being so loving, for your daily provisions, for your protection, and for using us when we do not deserve it. Thank you for your life in me!

8

WHEN JOY IS EXTINGUISHED

SCRIPTURE
Philippians 1:4

DEVOTIONAL REFLECTION
Paul is writing to the Philippians from a prison that is probably humid and likely full of cockroaches. He has almost no food, is probably ill, and yet he still says that he always prays with joy.

Joy is not a feeling. Joy is part of the fruit of the Holy Spirit. When we understand this, we realize that it is essential for God to fill us. Therefore, joy does not depend on our circumstances but, rather, on the relationship we have with God through Jesus Christ, which manifests itself in the fruit of the Spirit. If there is no prayer with joy, there is no day of joy.

Our dependence on God is key, for everything we have to do must be done with joy, even if we do not want to do it.

Joy is like a soothing oil for the spiritual, physical, and relational life. Joy is contagious even in the midst of hopeless situations, tribulations, and temptations. A genuine church possesses an air of joy that attracts people. What is the diagnosis of the absence of joy? (We are not talking about the feeling of happiness but about the fruit of the Spirit.)

As Christians, we cannot say that joy is possible if it does not manifest itself in our own lives.

SCRIPTURAL CONTEXT
Restore to me the joy of your salvation and grant me a willing spirit, to sustain me. (Psalm 51:12)

And the disciples were filled with joy and with the Holy Spirit. (Acts 13:52)

That is why, for Christ's sake, I delight in weaknesses, in insults, in hardships, in persecutions, in difficulties. For when I am weak, then I am strong. (2 Corinthians 12:10)

The faith and love that spring from the hope stored up for you in heaven and about which you have already heard in the true message of the gospel. (Colossians 1:5)

You became imitators of us and of the Lord, for you welcomed the message in the midst of severe suffering with the joy given by the Holy Spirit. (1 Thessalonians 1:6)

Fixing our eyes on Jesus, the pioneer and perfecter of faith. For the joy set before him he endured the cross, scorning its shame, and sat down at the right hand of the throne of God. (Hebrews 12:2)

For Further Study
Isaiah 62:5
Acts 20:24
Romans 14:17
Galatians 5:22–23
Colossians 1:24

JOURNAL

Make a list of situations, people, and activities that irritate you. Pray for all of them and ask God to give you joy in your heart as you face them.

_____

_____

_____

_____

_____

_____

_____

_____

_____

_____

_____

_____

_____

_____

_____

_____

_____

_____

_____

_____

_____

_____

_____

_____

_____

_____

_____

_____

PRAYER

Lord, help us to always pray for others when we remember them, whether they are people we like or people who have harmed us. Help us pray in thanksgiving for our circumstances, whatever they may be. But more than anything, help us pray with joy!

9 ∼

Intimate Communion

Scripture
Philippians 1:5

Devotional Reflection

Communion, *koinonia*, means participation. It is the voluntary act of contributing to or being part of something. *Koinonia* is to be the companion of someone on a mission, becoming the participant of a purpose that is more elevated than our highest ideals and goals.

Paul prays for the Philippians that they will be involved and be participants in the gospel. His prayer is for them to become active in announcing the good news of the love and sacrifice of Christ. This prayer is a call to the Philippians to not waste even one moment, circumstance, or occasion with another person to proclaim what Christ has done for them. It is a radical calling to evangelize!

Koinonia among Christians is more than being together to have a good time or enjoy the fellowship of others, even though that is a good part of communion. The essence of *koinonia* is complete participation in the nature of God as we adopt the life, character, and behavior of Christ. It is a calling to participate in his ministry, to participate in his power, and—above all—to participate in his death. Believers enter into *koinonia* when they decide to surrender to the will of God, and not to live for themselves, having intimate communion with Jesus—that is, with God himself.

Sometimes even church activities stop making Christ the priority. In that very moment, the communion with God is lost. It is not worth it to do or achieve anything without the presence of God with us.

Scriptural Context

Now if we are children, then we are heirs—heirs of God and co-heirs with Christ, if indeed we share in his sufferings in order that we may also share in his glory. (Romans 8:17)

God is faithful, who has called you into fellowship with his Son, Jesus Christ our Lord. (1 Corinthians 1:9)

I do all this for the sake of the gospel, that I may share in its blessings. (1 Corinthians 9:23)

May the grace of the Lord Jesus Christ, and the love of God, and the fellowship of the Holy Spirit be with you all. (2 Corinthians 13:14)

Through these he has given us his very great and precious promises, so that through them you may participate in the divine nature, having escaped the corruption in the world caused by evil desires. (2 Peter 1:4)

For Further Study
John 17:20–23
Philippians 1:7
Philippians 2:1
Philippians 3:10

Journal

Read all the passages in the Scriptural Context section. In each reading, notice when the word *communion* or the concept of communion (fellowship, sharing) is expressed. Write about the ways that Scripture indicates we can have intimate communion with God.

_____

_____

_____

_____

_____

_____

_____

_____

_____

_____

_____

_____

_____

_____

_____

_____

_____

_____

_____

_____

_____

_____

_____

_____

_____

_____

_____

_____

PRAYER

Father, thank you for allowing us to be coworkers and collaborators (1 Corinthians 3:9). Thank you for the fellowship of participating in the redemptive mission. Thank you because, as we have communion with you, we are "the pleasing aroma of Christ among those who are being saved and those who are perishing" (2 Corinthians 2:15).

10

UNCHANGEABLE CONVICTIONS

SCRIPTURE
Philippians 1:6

DEVOTIONAL REFLECTION

Paul has a personal conviction that comes from God. His conviction comes from his experience with Christ in the past, but it is also present, and he expresses it with the security that his conviction will continue. Paul's conviction is not just something related to reason or a mental belief of biblical truths. His conviction is the witness of the Holy Spirit of what God has done in him through Jesus Christ and of the continued work of God in his life. The conviction and security of always having in mind that God is God only comes from the inner witness of the Holy Spirit in our heart.

Faith in Christ and the conviction and security of our salvation and sanctification cannot sustain themselves on emotions, on reason, on responses to prayers, or even on being witness of miracles. Conviction and security come from the internal witness of the Holy Spirit in our hearts.

The only thing that sustains Paul is the conviction that God is real, and that God is the one who sustains Paul and gives him hope. God, and only God, is the one who motivates Paul to write letters to continue his calling and ministry even in a place from which it seems impossible to minister effectively.

Let us be sure that our faith is anchored in a genuine experience of salvation and sanctification, in which the Holy Spirit has witnessed to us that we are his children and he has purified us by faith in our hearts.

Scriptural Context

Then Agrippa said to Paul, "Do you think that in such a short time you can persuade me to be a Christian?" Paul replied, "Short time or long—I pray to God that not only you but all who are listening to me today may become what I am, except for these chains." (Acts 26:28–29)

The Spirit himself testifies with our spirit that we are God's children. (Romans 8:16)

My message and my preaching were not with wise and persuasive words, but with a demonstration of the Spirit's power, so that your faith might not rest on human wisdom, but on God's power. (1 Corinthians 2:4–5)

Since, then, we know what it is to fear the Lord, we try to persuade others. What we are is plain to God, and I hope it is also plain to your conscience. (2 Corinthians 5:11)

For Further Study
Acts 15:8–9
Acts 28:23
Romans 8:38–39
2 Corinthians 3:4–6
Ephesians 3:10–13

Journal

What is your motivation when things do not happen as you expected? Write down a personal creed, including the convictions that God has given you, that are the basis of your peace, joy, and security that God will always be present.

_____

_____

_____

_____

_____

_____

_____

_____

_____

_____

_____

_____

_____

_____

_____

_____

_____

_____

_____

_____

_____

_____

_____

_____

_____

PRAYER

Lord, thank you for anchoring our faith in the witness of your Holy Spirit to our hearts. Thank you for giving us profound and solid convictions even in the midst of unforeseen and impossible circumstances like the ones the apostle Paul faced.

11

BEGINNING OF BEGINNINGS

SCRIPTURE
Philippians 1:6

DEVOTIONAL REFLECTION

The word "began" (*enarchomai*) is a compound word between *en*, a preposition that means "a position with the capacity of," and *archomai*, which means "to govern or start something." The one who began the good work in us is God. He has power, authority to do whatever he wants out of nothing. The one who began always makes everything new. God is a specialist in beginnings and new opportunities.

In Christ, everything is new! It is not about money, social position, or a place in leadership; it is about being in Christ Jesus.

How many times do we hear people say, "If I could only start all over again"? Today you can make the decision not to torture yourself anymore with the guilt from the past. Ask for forgiveness and allow Christ to reign in your heart so that everything will be made new. You can be born again!

Paul is convinced that God is the God of beginnings. The apostle has experienced a new birth, a new spiritual life. Here there are no halfways. God makes it new! Paul has experienced many circumstances in which God has helped him start again. God helps Paul take the gospel to new cities, start new churches, and gain new converts and new disciples.

Every morning in Christ, in the power of the Holy Spirit, is a new opportunity, a new beginning. The new life in Christ is never our own initiative. It is God's initiative. Today God is looking for people in order to make them new, to give them new life. The key is that God uses us as heralds to announce that he wants to do something new.

Scriptural Context

Because of the LORD's great love we are not consumed, for his compassions never fail. They are new every morning; great is your faithfulness. (Lamentations 3:22–23)

Therefore, if anyone is in Christ, the new creation has come: The old has gone, the new is here! (2 Corinthians 5:17)

For it is by grace you have been saved, through faith—and this is not from yourselves, it is the gift of God—not by works, so that no one can boast. For we are God's handiwork, created in Christ Jesus to do good works, which God prepared in advance for us to do. (Ephesians 2:8–10)

For Further Study
John 6:29
1 Corinthians 1:8
Philippians 2:13

Journal

Do you feel like you need a new opportunity in your life? Write down all the new aspects of your life since you started to follow Christ as his disciple. Write down some circumstances and new opportunities you've had since Christ saved and forgave you. Give thanks to God for those things.

_____

_____

_____

_____

_____

_____

_____

_____

_____

_____

_____

_____

_____

_____

_____

_____

_____

_____

_____

_____

_____

_____

PRAYER

Thank you, Lord, for each new opportunity. Thank you for having
started all over in me and giving me a new life in Christ. Thank you,
Lord, for giving us something new each day, a new hope. Thank you
for being the God of grace, peace, and mercy. We praise you and
glorify you for being so good to us.

12 ❧
THE EXCELLENT WORK

SCRIPTURE
Philippians 1:6

DEVOTIONAL REFLECTION
Paul is sure that God has started something new in the Philippians. What God does is not only new; it is good! To say the truth, it is done with excellence! There is nothing mediocre or evil in what God does. God started a good work. It is a work of grace. What he does is free, new, and good.

When God finds us, he applies to our lives the marvelous, costly, free work that our Lord Jesus Christ performed on the cross of Calvary for each person who has existed. We are the recipients of the great work of God! What a privilege!

What God has started in your life, he will continue to perfect in your ministry. He is not a God who leaves things halfway done! We were evil in nature, but now God has done something new and good! He has begun a new work.

We have to consider that our new life in Christ, the new birth, is the good work of God in our life. In ourselves we are not good; it is he in us who does good. It is through the power of the Holy Spirit in our lives that we can do what is good. Only God receives the glory for our lives, for what we are and what we do.

SCRIPTURAL CONTEXT
"Why do you ask me about what is good?" Jesus replied. "There is only One who is good." (Matthew 19:17a)

For everything God created is good. (1 Timothy 4:4a)

Dear friend, do not imitate what is evil but what is good. Anyone who does what is good is from God. Anyone who does what is evil has not seen God. (3 John 1:11)

For Further Study
Genesis 1:1–31
Ephesians 2:1–5

JOURNAL
Describe some radical changes that God has done in your life.

_____

_____

_____

_____

_____

_____

_____

_____

_____

_____

_____

_____

_____

_____

_____

PRAYER
Lord, thank you, thank you, thank you. Thank you for doing a new and good work in our lives, and thank you because you will work in us until the last day.

13

GOD CONTINUES TO WORK IN MY LIFE

SCRIPTURE
Philippians 1:6

DEVOTIONAL REFLECTION

The phrase "will carry it on to completion" is a Greek compound: *epiteleo. Epi* means "over, around;" *teleo* means "achievement, success, perfecting, fulfilled purpose." That is what the work of God is like—over us and around us, fulfilling the purpose for which he created us.

Paul says to the Philippians that the God, who is the Creator, the Almighty, did, through the work of Christ, a good and new work. He tells them that God "has begun," which means God will continue to work and labor in us to perfect us. God's salvation in our lives is a process with key events on the way.

First, God makes us conscious that we are sinners. Then he saves us because of his love and grace. When we are born again, he gives us his Holy Spirit. Then he purifies our intentions and cleanses our hearts from our self-sovereignty, filling us with his Holy Spirit and his love. Once we are full of him, he starts to show us issues that we have from our past life, issues of a damaged personality, ways of speaking and saying things, habits, etc. It is in the measure that we concentrate on him that his image continues to be formed in us.

Then we start to shine in a world of darkness. God reveals to us those things that we carry from our old lives so we can leave them behind and shine. The problem is when we do not want to submit to his lordship and do not surrender 100 percent. God will continue to work in our lives as long as we live. Even when our heads are full of gray hair and our legs need the help of a cane, God continues to mold us. Let us allow the divine Potter to continue to form us into his image. Let us keep our clay malleable, allowing his hands to touch us and shape us.

This good and new work of his will continue to be perfected "until the day of Christ Jesus." The day of Christ Jesus is his second coming. God will redeem the whole of creation we have contaminated and damaged. What a marvelous process! The cost—the life of Jesus Christ—was incredible, but the results—complete transformation—are incomparable.

SCRIPTURAL CONTEXT

God, who knows the heart, showed that he accepted them by giving the Holy Spirit to them, just as he did to us. He did not discriminate between us and them, for he purified their hearts by faith. (Acts 15:8–9)

And we all, who with unveiled faces contemplate the Lord's glory, are being transformed into his image with ever-increasing glory, which comes from the Lord, who is the Spirit. (2 Corinthians 3:18)

Therefore, since we have these promises, dear friends, let us purify ourselves from everything that contaminates body and spirit, perfecting holiness out of reverence for God. (2 Corinthians 7:1)

May God himself, the God of peace, sanctify you through and through. May your whole spirit, soul and body be kept blameless at the coming of our Lord Jesus Christ. (1 Thessalonians 5:23)

Praise be to the God and Father of our Lord Jesus Christ! In his great mercy he has given us new birth into a living hope through the resurrection of Jesus Christ from the dead. (1 Peter 1:3)

For Further Study
John 19:30
2 Corinthians 4:6–7
Philippians 3:13–14
1 Peter 1:8–9
Revelation 21:6–7

JOURNAL

Is there an area in your personality that is preventing others from seeing Christ in you? Write about it and ask God, by his grace, to show you how to change that area that has not been perfected in your life.

_____

_____

_____

_____

_____

_____

_____

_____

_____

_____

_____

_____

_____

_____

_____

_____

_____

_____

_____

_____

PRAYER

Lord, open my mind, examine me, and continue to touch aspects of my life so I can continue to grow each day more and more in your image.

14
PARTICIPANTS IN GRACE

SCRIPTURE
Philippians 1:7

DEVOTIONAL REFLECTION
Paul writes this letter to his readers full of expressions of joy from prison. He also talks about defending and confirming the gospel. He doesn't talk about his own defense, or about demanding his rights, or about seeking his own benefit. Paul's passions are the gospel, his disciples, and the lost. Paul is centered in Christ and others. He gave up his own self.

Discipleship is key for Paul. Paul makes the Philippians conscious of the benefit of God's grace, and leads them to be active disciples by that same grace.

The key word in the whole letter to the Philippians is "feel." However, this does not refer to an emotion. The word "feel" in this context means "to think with purpose."

The climax verse, which is also the axis verse in Philippians, is 2:5. Paul has the same mindset as Christ Jesus and possesses the mind of Christ. That is the reason he has the Philippians in his heart, and he makes them co-participants in the grace of Christ.

SCRIPTURAL CONTEXT
Do you not know? Have you not heard? The LORD is the everlasting God, the Creator of the ends of the earth. He will not grow tired or weary, and his understanding no one can fathom. (Isaiah 40:28)

Dear brothers and sisters, I close my letter with these last words: Be joyful. Grow to maturity. Encourage each other. Live in harmony and peace. Then the God of love and peace will be with you. (2 Corinthians 13:11, NLT)

Then make my joy complete by being like-minded, having the same love, being one in spirit and of one mind. (Philippians 2:2)

You must have the same attitude that Christ Jesus had. (Philippians 2:5, NLT)

JOURNAL

What kind of letter would you write in Paul's place? In the following lines, write a brief note of encouragement to someone and pray for him or her.

_____

_____

_____

_____

_____

_____

_____

_____

_____

_____

_____

_____

_____

_____

_____

PRAYER

Father, we give you thanks for giving us the mind of Christ, the love of your Son, the same mindset, and the same purpose. Help us decrease so that you may increase so that many can receive the salvation you have in store for them.

15 ❧
WITNESS?

SCRIPTURE
Philippians 1:8

DEVOTIONAL REFLECTION

Paul invokes the idea of God being his witness in order to declare that God knows the depths of his heart. Placing God as a witness is common for the people of the Old Testament.

Is it correct to place God as a witness? It is truly something very serious because we are calling on God to ratify what we say, what we do, and who we are. It is like the child who says to his dad that he hasn't had candy but has candy smeared on his face. Even though the external evidence might not be as clear as that, God knows everything because God sees our inner selves.

When the Holy Spirit comes to our lives, he gives witness to our spirit that we are saved (Romans 8:16); and when we are consecrated, he gives witness that we have been purified by faith (Acts 15:8–9). But when he comes in his fullness, he does not only witness to our spirit; he makes us witnesses to others of the wonders of God (Acts 1:8). Jesus said that the Spirit would witness about him to others (see John 16).

I can only make God my witness when the Holy Spirit has witnessed the two works of grace in my life. Otherwise, I would be lying. I can only be God's witness when he has made me his witness with the infilling of the Holy Spirit. It is then and only then that I can say, "God can testify . . ."

The Bible says Jesus is the faithful witness. Our witness is based on his witness about us, him living in us and through us. A witness is someone who has seen an act or event and, in many instances, can define the situation of others. Being witnesses of Jesus can change the direction of people's lives.

SCRIPTURAL CONTEXT

"You are a king, then!" said Pilate. Jesus answered, "You say that I am a king. In fact, the reason I was born and came into the world is to testify to the truth. Everyone on the side of truth listens to me." (John 18:37)

"When the Advocate comes, whom I will send to you from the Father—the Spirit of truth who goes out from the Father—he will testify about me." (John 15:26)

But you will receive power when the Holy Spirit comes on you; and you will be my witnesses in Jerusalem, and in all Judea and Samaria, and to the ends of the earth. (Acts 1:8)

You know we never used flattery, nor did we put on a mask to cover up greed—God is our witness. We were not looking for praise from people, not from you or anyone else, even though as apostles of Christ we could have asserted our authority. (1 Thessalonians 2:5–6)

To the angel of the church in Laodicea write: These are the words of the Amen, the faithful and true witness, the ruler of God's creation. (Revelation 3:14)

For Further Study
John 8:14–15
Acts 15:8–9
Romans 1:9
Romans 8:16
2 Corinthians 1:23

JOURNAL

Can you place God as a witness of the love you feel for others? And of your service to him?

Explain in your words what the witness of the Spirit is in the life of a believer (see Romans 8:16) and in the life that is full of the Holy Spirit (see Acts 15:8–9).

_____

_____

_____

_____

_____

_____

_____

_____

_____

_____

_____

_____

_____

_____

_____

_____

_____

_____

PRAYER

Lord, witness to our hearts through your Spirit. Make us witnesses of your presence in our lives and of your wonders. Make us truthful witnesses of you before a world that needs to see you.

16
WITNESSES OF WHAT?

SCRIPTURE
Philippians 1:8

DEVOTIONAL REFLECTION
Paul says God is witness to the fact that Paul loves the Philippians with the love of Jesus Christ. It is important to notice that Paul does not love them with his own love but with the enduring love of Jesus Christ. He is saying that he loves them from the deepest part of his being. We call enduring love the love of a mother, for mothers carry their babies inside themselves. Paul is using the same image: *The love of God is mine; I carry it in the deepest part of myself. It is the love of Jesus Christ!*

On our own strength, we cannot love like God loves, to the point of giving up our most precious treasure to save others. We can love— but not to the point of surrendering what we love the most. Only when the Holy Spirit is poured in our hearts can we love God and our neighbors. The lack of love toward our neighbors is the greatest obstacle that exists for our prayers to get to God.

I ask myself if all the brothers and sisters in Philippi really deserve Paul's enduring love. However, regardless of what they deserve, he can offer it because the Holy Spirit has been poured out into his heart.

Ask God for the capacity to love everyone equally. A brave person is the one who loves no matter if they are loved in return. A brave person is someone who can exercise self-control against injustices and who does not take vengeance.

God gives us a spirit of power to be more than victorious!

Scriptural Context

Help us, God our Savior, for the glory of your name; deliver us and forgive our sins for your name's sake. (Psalm 79:9)

And hope does not put us to shame, because God's love has been poured out into our hearts through the Holy Spirit, who has been given to us. (Romans 5:5)

I pray that out of his glorious riches he may strengthen you with power through his Spirit in your inner being, so that Christ may dwell in your hearts through faith. And I pray that you, being rooted and established in love, may have power, together with all the Lord's holy people, to grasp how wide and long and high and deep is the love of Christ, and to know this love that surpasses knowledge—that you may be filled to the measure of all the fullness of God. (Ephesians 3:16–19)

For Further Study
John 5:42
Romans 5:8
Romans 8:39
2 Corinthians 13:14
2 Thessalonians 3:5
2 Timothy 1:7

Journal

Describe a situation in which you have exercised love with power, with courage, and with self-discipline. What was the result of your love?

_____

_____

_____

_____

_____

_____

_____

_____

_____

_____

_____

_____

_____

_____

_____

_____

_____

_____

_____

_____

_____

_____

_____

_____

_____

_____

_____

_____

_____

PRAYER

Our Father, I beg you to continue to pour down your love in our hearts, and toward everyone around us. Love them through us, through your Holy Spirit. Give us your mindset, your compassion, and your love to take your salvation and comfort to brothers and sisters and to those who do not know you yet. Allow us to see you, love you, and serve you with all our strength.

17 ❧
BIBLICAL PROSPERITY

SCRIPTURE
Philippians 1:9

DEVOTIONAL REFLECTION
The priority in Paul's request is for the Philippians to abound more and more in love. Why should we abound more and more in love? Because it is God's desire for us to be filled with him. To be filled with the love of God, we need to receive the infilling of the Holy Spirit.

Only the love of God flowing in our life will demonstrate who God is in each area of our lives. Love is dynamic. It is not static. We can strengthen it, or we can ignore it until it disappears from our hearts. We need to develop it, nurture it, and increase it.

The purpose of love is for everyone to know that we are disciples of Jesus.

SCRIPTURAL CONTEXT
A new command I give you: Love one another. As I have loved you, so you must love one another. By this everyone will know that you are my disciples, if you love one another. (John 13:34–35)

So it is with you. Since you are eager for gifts of the Spirit, try to excel in those that build up the church. (1 Corinthians 14:12)

May the Lord make your love increase and overflow for each other and for everyone else, just as ours does for you. (1 Thessalonians 3:12)

Dear friends, let us love one another, for love comes from God. Everyone who loves has been born of God and knows God. Whoever does not love does not know God, because God is love. (1 John 4:7–8)

For Further Study
1 Corinthians 13:1–13
1 John 5:3

JOURNAL

What does the word *prosperity* mean to you? How does Paul define biblical prosperity? How is the concept of prosperity in our society different from the concept of prosperity in the Bible?

_____

_____

_____

_____

_____

_____

_____

_____

_____

_____

_____

_____

_____

PRAYER

Lord, prosper us in love! Fill us until we overflow with your love to give it out to a world that desperately seeks real love, unconditional love, love that suffers, your love. Help us to pour out our lives with love to others, to present your love through our attitudes, our actions, our words, and our deeds. Open our eyes to see the needs of others, and allow us to love them with your love.

18

ABUNDANT INSIGHT AND KNOWLEDGE

SCRIPTURE
Philippians 1:9

DEVOTIONAL REFLECTION

"Knowledge" in this passage means complete discernment; "depth of insight" also references discernment. Paul prays that the love of God that dwells in the hearts of the Philippians will help them discern what is and what is not from God. He desires that the love of God will help them base their discernment on the Word of God.

The only person who has all knowledge (discernment) is God. To discern is to distinguish between what is true and what is false. The profound knowledge of who God is will help us know immediately what is false.

Abounding "more and more" implies a personal effort of not becoming content with what one already has. More and more is the practice of the discipline of concentrating on him.

Mental knowledge is very important, but if it is not saturated with the love of God, it turns into pride and arrogance.

The knowledge of God helps us recognize that God is the source of everything. It places us on our proper level and helps us know what the will of God is for our lives.

God gives discernment for us to know the truth and for it to be manifested through our holy lives!

SCRIPTURAL CONTEXT

May my cry come before you, LORD; give me understanding according to your word. (Psalm 119:169)

Indeed, if you call out for insight and cry aloud for understanding, and if you look for it as for silver and search for it as for hidden treasure, then you will understand the fear of the LORD and find the knowledge of God. For the LORD gives wisdom; from his mouth come knowledge and understanding. (Proverbs 2:3–6)

And we all, who with unveiled faces contemplate the Lord's glory, are being transformed into his image with ever-increasing glory, which comes from the Lord, who is the Spirit. (2 Corinthians 3:18)

For Further Study
Psalm 119:97–99
Proverbs 3:13–15
1 Corinthians 14:20
Ephesians 5:17–18

JOURNAL

What do you understand about discernment? What can you do daily for the love of God in you to abound more and more in knowledge and depth of insight? Use the verses from the Scriptural Context section to guide you in your response.

_____

_____

_____

_____

_____

_____

_____

_____

_____

_____

_____

_____

_____

_____

_____

_____

_____

_____

_____

_____

_____

_____

_____

_____

_____

_____

_____

_____

_____

_____

_____

_____

_____

_____

_____

_____

_____

_____

PRAYER

Lord, we want more of you, more of your love. We want to know you better so that when something before us is not from you, we can walk away from it and have the discernment to live in holiness.

19

POSITIVE CONSEQUENCES

SCRIPTURE

Philippians 1:9–10

DEVOTIONAL REFLECTION

What is the fruit of love that abounds in the knowledge of God and discernment? Paul answers that such love chooses what is best. Another version says what is excellent. The love and knowledge of God abounding in our lives helps us not conform to mediocrity but to follow the way of excellence. Excellence is the fruit of a life that is surrendered to God that chooses discipline, healthy and elevated habits, and transparency in everything. When this happens in our lives, we give a genuine witness to the work of God.

The Christian life is not a momentary or passing experience. It is a continual and constant walk with Christ. The Christian life is the discipline of knowing God, knowing his mind, being transformed by his Word, and making responsible decisions that will affect us, our surroundings, and everyone around us who will receive the consequences of our decisions.

For how long? Until "the day of Christ," that is, the day of his second coming, or the day of our death.

SCRIPTURAL CONTEXT

But if serving the LORD seems undesirable to you, then choose for yourselves this day whom you will serve, whether the gods your ancestors served beyond the Euphrates, or the gods of the Amorites, in whose land you are living. But as for me and my household, we will serve the LORD. (Joshua 24:15)

Do not conform to the pattern of this world, but be transformed by the renewing of your mind. Then you will be able to test and approve what God's will is—his good, pleasing and perfect will. (Romans 12:2)

We put no stumbling block in anyone's path, so that our ministry will not be discredited. (2 Corinthians 6:3)

And find out what pleases the Lord. Have nothing to do with the fruitless deeds of darkness, but rather expose them. (Ephesians 5:10–11)

JOURNAL

Write down some spiritual habits that would help you choose the best so that you may be pure and blameless for the day of Christ.

_____

_____

_____

_____

_____

_____

_____

_____

_____

_____

_____

_____

_____

_____

_____

_____

_____

_____

PRAYER

Lord, answer today Paul's prayer in our lives. Help us abound in love, knowledge, and discernment so we can be excellent Christians who are responsible, disciplined, and making a difference today.

20 ❧
LIVING BASKETS, FULL OF FRUIT

SCRIPTURE
Philippians 1:11

DEVOTIONAL REFLECTION
Paul has prayed for the Philippians that the love of God will abound in them and that they will be firm until the second coming of the Lord Jesus Christ. Now he tells them that as they wait for the coming of the Lord Jesus Christ, they need to be "filled with the fruit of righteousness," or fruits of rectitude and justice.

Fruit in the Bible is always identified with the presence of the Holy Spirit in the believer. At the end of the prayer (Philippians 1:8–11), Paul presents the action of the Trinity: He tells them that the fruit of righteousness [of the Spirit], is through Jesus Christ, and for the glory and praise of God.

The only way to be filled with the fruit of righteousness (justice) is to abide in Jesus, in radical obedience to his Word. It is the only way of bearing fruit (the fruit of the Spirit), more fruit (disciples), much fruit (the disciples of our disciples), and fruit that remains (disciples involved in ministry according to their gifts and abilities).

SCRIPTURAL CONTEXT
Blessed is the one who does not walk in step with the wicked or stand in the way that sinners take or sit in the company of mockers, but whose delight is in the law of the LORD, and who meditates on his law day and night. That person is like a tree planted by streams of water, which yields its fruit in season and whose leaf does not wither—whatever they do prosper. (Psalm 1:1–3)

I am the vine; you are the branches. If you remain in me and I in you, you will bear much fruit; apart from me you can do nothing. (John 15:5)

This is to my Father's glory, that you bear much fruit, showing yourselves to be my disciples. (John 15:8)

You did not choose me, but I chose you and appointed you so that you might go and bear fruit—fruit that will last—and so that whatever you ask in my name the Father will give you. (John 15:16)

For Further Study
Psalm 92:12–15
John 15:7
Romans 6:22
Galatians 5:22–23
Ephesians 5:9–10
Hebrews 12:11

JOURNAL

Make a list of your fruit: a) fruit of the Spirit (Galatians 5:22–23); b) more fruit (the people God has given you to disciple); c) the multiplication of disciples through your disciples; and d) fruit that remains (the disciples already in ministry or work at a local church).

_____

_____

_____

_____

_____

_____

_____

_____

_____

_____

_____

_____

_____

_____

_____

_____

_____

_____

_____

_____

_____

_____

_____

_____

_____

_____

_____

_____

_____

_____

_____

_____

_____

_____

PRAYER

Lord, give us the fruit of righteousness. Give us a character that is full of righteousness to think on others as your love abounds more and more in us. Thank you for always being consistent and for always loving us in spite of our mistakes. Allow our fruit to abound.

21 ❧
SPREADING THE NEWS

SCRIPTURE
Philippians 1:12

DEVOTIONAL REFLECTION

The expression "I want you to know" is very strong. It is an intense desire that Paul has not to hide anything that is happening to him. He has been maliciously accused and has ended up in a Roman prison where food is scarce. He has found himself in inhumane conditions. Paul's calling is to be a missionary (an apostle, a sent one). He thought he would go to the ends of the earth; his idea was to get to Spain. However, he ends up in a prison cell. But in spite of his suffering, a prison does not take away his missionary calling.

Today, through his letters written from prison, we have received the message through all kinds of massive media, electronics, and so on. Paul still communicates and ministers today, and to the ends of the earth! Difficult circumstances do not stop the work of God; even though sometimes it feels like everything is lost, we can be surprised by the Father.

Paul wants us to know that everything that has happened—with God's permission, but without being caused by God—has "actually served to advance the gospel." Paul's enterprise has resulted in the best dividends of history. Examining the success of the gospel of Jesus Christ, today proclaimed for almost two thousand years to millions of people, and literally to the ends of the earth, we have the certainty that nothing, nobody, and no circumstance can ever stop the gospel.

Paul wants to proclaim in a loud voice the success of the gospel ("I want you to know"). We should not be ashamed of the clear and biblical message of salvation; this will produce fruit, more fruit, much fruit, and fruit that remains (see John 15).

Investing everything we have in the gospel is the best enterprise we can have. It may not produce a financial dividend. We could end up in a filthy prison cell, "but the word of the Lord endures forever. And this is the word that was preached to you" (1 Peter 1:25).

SCRIPTURAL CONTEXT

Your word, LORD, is eternal; it stands firm in the heavens. (Psalm 119:89)

The grass withers and the flowers fall, but the word of our God endures forever. (Isaiah 40:8)

Remember Jesus Christ, raised from the dead, descended from David. This is my gospel, for which I am suffering even to the point of being chained like a criminal. But God's word is not chained. (2 Timothy 2:8–9)

For Further Study
Exodus 18:11
Deuteronomy 8:2–3
Psalm 46:1–3
Romans 1:16
Romans 5:3–5
Romans 8:28–29

JOURNAL

What are you investing your life in? In the following lines, make a calendar for the next three days that explains how you will invest your life in the propagation of the gospel.

_____

_____

_____

_____

_____

_____

_____

_____

_____

_____

_____

_____

_____

_____

_____

_____

_____

_____

_____

_____

_____

_____

_____

_____

_____

_____

_____

_____

_____

_____

_____

PRAYER

Thank you, Lord, for making us co-participants in the best of tasks, the best of investments—proclaiming who you are, proclaiming your great love, and sharing your great salvation. There is not a better way to invest our lives!

22

I Cannot Go Unnoticed

Scripture

Philippians 1:13

All the soldiers here, and everyone else, too, found out that I'm in jail because of this Messiah. (MSG)

Devotional Reflection

The most famous verse of the Bible, John 3:16, begins with John saying that God loved the world in a way that was so incredible that he gave Jesus Christ, his only Son, as a sacrifice for the salvation of all humanity. Now Paul speaks of the repercussions of the gospel and of the preaching of the good news of John 3:16. Even though he is in prison, the gospel has caused an earthquake with repercussions. And it is in such a way that what was perpetrated for evil has turned to be good: Prison has served to give public witness of Christ.

Paul has won over his prison guard to Christ. He is under the custody of four guards made up of four soldiers each, a total of twenty-four hours a day. Paul makes the name of Christ famous throughout the whole palace guard. And not only does Paul make him famous, but now, Jesus is an intimate friend of "those who belong to Caesar's household." Paul has introduced them! Paul also wins other prisoners to the cause of Christ. The prison can enchain Paul, but it cannot enchain the good news of the Lord Jesus Christ.

A person full of the Holy Spirit sees adversity as opportunities to give public witness of Christ to the people (Philippians 1:13). Adversities are not for us to feel self-pity; they are there for our needs to become a trampoline to present Christ to those who see our need.

Scriptural Context

And pray in the Spirit on all occasions with all kinds of prayers and requests. With this in mind, be alert and always keep on praying for all the Lord's people. Pray also for me, that whenever I speak, words may be given me so that I will fearlessly make known the mystery of the gospel, for which I am an ambassador in chains. Pray that I may declare it fearlessly, as I should. (Ephesians 6:18–20)

The Lord's message rang out from you not only in Macedonia and Achaia—your faith in God has become known everywhere. Therefore we do not need to say anything about it, for they themselves report what kind of reception you gave us. They tell how you turned to God from idols to serve the living and true God. (1 Thessalonians 1:8–9)

For Further Study
Acts 28:16
1 Peter 4:12–16

JOURNAL

What do you do in the midst of adversities? Do you start to argue, complain, or allow bitterness to pollute your heart? In what ways are you redirecting your circumstances for the expansion of the gospel?

_____

_____

_____

_____

_____

_____

_____

_____

PRAYER

Lord, help me see my surroundings—those closest to me, the people I know, those you place near me whom I do not know—and help me so love them that they may come to know that Jesus died for them, and that everything may be used to advance your kingdom.

23

RESULTS OF BEING FOCUSED ON THE MISSION (1)

SCRIPTURE
Philippians 1:14

DEVOTIONAL REFLECTION

The word *confident* is key and in the secular world means courage or daring. But here it is even stronger because it is confident *in the Lord.* The brothers and sisters find themselves in the Lord. Their confidence and courage do not depend on the situation of Paul; they depend on the fact that they are in the Lord.

Paul is focused on fulfilling the mission of Jesus Christ, and this has cost him his freedom. But his chains are like a fuel for others, as we see in Philippians 1:14. Paul's love for God continues to cause repercussions. The key of the Christian life is where we are. We can be concentrated on ourselves, or we can live in the Lord. Notice that the brothers and sisters are not proclaiming what is happening to Paul; they are speaking the Word without fear.

Even though our witness can encourage others, if it is not accompanied by good preaching from the Bible, it will not produce results. We can say that witnessing is the first step, and then comes the Word of God. If you want to be a Christian who produces results—that is, one who impacts others—the Bible has to be your main source, your spiritual food. Even though there are many self-help books and different programs to follow, nothing can replace the Bible; after all, nobody can proclaim something they do not know.

SCRIPTURAL CONTEXT

Praise be to the God and Father of our Lord Jesus Christ, the Father of compassion and the God of all comfort, who comforts us in all our troubles, so that we can comfort those in any trouble with the comfort we ourselves receive from God. For just as we share abundantly in the sufferings of Christ, so also our comfort abounds through Christ. If we are distressed, it is for your comfort and salvation; if we are comforted, it is for your comfort, which produces in you patient endurance of the same sufferings we suffer. And our hope for you is firm, because we know that just as you share in our sufferings, so also you share in our comfort. (2 Corinthians 1:3–7)

We had previously suffered and been treated outrageously in Philippi, as you know, but with the help of our God we dared to tell you his gospel in the face of strong opposition. (1 Thessalonians 2:2)

JOURNAL

Write a promise specifying which portions of the Bible you will read in the next three days.

_____

_____

_____

_____

_____

_____

_____

_____

_____

_____

PRAYER

Lord help us live in you, to know your Word deeply, and to proclaim it without fear. We pray for those Christians who are in prison today. Thank you for their example and the confidence that encourage us to continue preaching the message of salvation.

24

RESULTS OF BEING FOCUSED ON THE MISSION (2)

SCRIPTURE
Philippians 1:15–18

DEVOTIONAL REFLECTION

The church is similar to a hospital where sick people come in to be healed of different illnesses. God makes our spirits to be born again and makes us new creatures in Christ. Many times, believers also receive healing from physical and mental illnesses. God also heals us of bad habits. God heals us in order that we can be part of the healthy body of Christ and start becoming an active part of the church, according to our gifts and talents, to advance the kingdom through the church of the Lord Jesus Christ.

However, sometimes people only make a mental decision and do not repent of their sins. They are not willing to radically obey God and his Word, and therefore they are not transformed; yet they continue to be in the church. Instead of being believers, followers, and disciples of Jesus Christ, they become religious. They have in some sense changed in form, but they have not changed internally. They have the Christian vocabulary, and a lot of their conduct is ethical but not all of it. They attend church, many become leaders in local churches, and some even become pastors. However, they have not really had a radical and transforming experience with the Lord Jesus Christ. Jesus talks about these people as weeds that his enemy plants. He says they grow within the church. Their fruit is visible—fruit of the flesh and fruit of darkness. That fruit is in the church, but it is not part of the kingdom!

Many others have been born again, but like the branches in the parable of the gardener, they are really not attached to the vine, and they are not nourished with the divine sap (see John 15).

The apostle Paul has enemies that appear to be more spiritual and more Christian than he is. If we are believers—followers and disciples of Christ—we will have these kind of enemies who preach Christ out of envy and rivalry, wanting to stir up trouble. If the enemies cause trouble, they overwhelm us and try to damage our balance. But we should not allow them to damage our spirit and our love of preaching the gospel. Jesus will come one day and separate us in the final trial. These enemies can actually be helpful, for they sharpen our capacity for patience, making us more transparent so that Christ may shine through us. On the other hand, the Bible says: "So is my word that goes out from my mouth: It will not return to me empty, but will accomplish what I desire and achieve the purpose for which I sent it" (Isaiah 55:11). Even though these people might have low motives, even though they might be double-minded, the gospel, the Word they preach, will not return empty.

As Paul says, the important thing is that Christ is preached. And because of that, Paul rejoices. Paul does not lose his joy, even with enemies who are trying to stir up trouble while he is in chains.

SCRIPTURAL CONTEXT

Everything they do is done for people to see: They make their phylacteries wide and the tassels on their garments long; they love the place of honor at banquets and the most important seats in the synagogues; they love to be greeted with respect in the marketplaces and to be called "Rabbi" by others. (Matthew 23:5–7)

I urge you, brothers and sisters, to watch out for those who cause divisions and put obstacles in your way that are contrary to the teaching you have learned. Keep away from them. For such people are not serving our Lord Christ, but their own appetites. By smooth talk and flattery they deceive the minds of naive people. (Romans 16:17–18)

For Further Study
Matthew 13:24–30

JOURNAL

Have you lost your joy because people in your church have treated you badly or been unfair with you? Make a private list of people who persecute you or have tried to harm you. In the following lines, write a prayer for them.

_____

_____

_____

_____

_____

_____

_____

_____

_____

_____

_____

_____

_____

_____

_____

_____

PRAYER

Lord, help us be part of the solution, not the problem. Help us be part of the wheat, not the weeds. Help us not to be full of bitterness but to remain in your joy, your fruit, the fruit of the Spirit. Help us bear abundant and healthy fruit for your honor and glory.

25

Prayer + Provision of the Spirit = Deliverance

Scripture

Philippians 1:19

Devotional Reflection

In the midst of his chains Paul has joy, but he also has hope. He trusts in God, but he also trusts others. He knows he is not alone. Paul has a confidence that is unchangeable. The phrase "For I know" is more than a mental affirmation. It is the conviction of the providence and prayer of the church for him. Paul presents a wonderful formula for each situation, whether it be an illness, bad habits, or people lost in sin. It is an effective formula based on hope. The formula is: Prayer + Provision of the Spirit = Deliverance.

The formula works in the following way: a) we pray for the needs of others; b) Jesus joins our prayer, interceding for us; c) the Holy Spirit prays with us and for us, interceding with wordless groans; d) the Father hears our prayer, that of Jesus, and that of the Holy Spirit, and acts according to his will. Paul calls steps b, c, and d "the provision of the Spirit of Jesus Christ."

This passage invites us to trust in our brothers and sisters—to trust in the church. It invites us to present our needs and the needs of others in public. On the other hand, it also calls for us to pray for the needs of others; to take them to the throne of grace to receive help for their needs. The result is incredible—deliverance. The result is the answer to prayer, and God receives the glory.

Scriptural Context

You brought us into prison and laid burdens on our backs. You let people ride over our heads; we went through fire and water, but you brought us to a place of abundance. (Psalm 66:11–12)

Therefore he is able to save completely those who come to God through him, because he always lives to intercede for them. (Hebrews 7:25)

Because you know that the testing of your faith produces perseverance. Let perseverance finish its work so that you may be mature and complete, not lacking anything. (James 1:3–4)

These have come so that the proven genuineness of your faith—of greater worth than gold, which perishes even though refined by fire—may result in praise, glory and honor when Jesus Christ is revealed. (1 Peter 1:7)

For Further Study
Proverbs 17:3
Romans 8:26–27
Hebrews 4:16

Journal

Choose four people you are praying for and follow the steps outlined in the Devotional Reflection. Then pray for the result. Write down the whole process in detail. Give thanks to God for the opportunity of praying for these people.

_____

_____

_____

_____

_____

_____

_____

_____

_____

_____

_____

_____

_____

_____

_____

_____

_____

_____

_____

_____

_____

_____

_____

_____

_____

_____

_____

_____

_____

_____

PRAYER

Lord, thank you for giving us such a wonderful hope to be able to trust in you. Thank you for the privilege of talking to the King of kings and Lord of lords, and being able to share our needs and the needs of others. Thank you for prayer. Thank you because you are with us and you minister to us in the Spirit as we pray. What a blessed privilege!

26
LIVING MAGNIFYING GLASSES

SCRIPTURE
Philippians 1:20

DEVOTIONAL REFLECTION

The words of Paul come from an unchangeable security in Jesus Christ: eagerly expect, hope, in no way ashamed, have sufficient courage, always. Who would imagine he is writing from a prison cell, knowing that his own execution might be near? Paul is suffering physically, but his joy, and the mission and purpose of his life, have not deteriorated at all.

His mission is always to magnify Christ in his body. Paul wants every attitude, every gesture, every thought, every response he gives, to show that Jesus Christ lives in him. Paul's confidence is not due to his worldly blessings (material goods, health, fame, etc.), for he doesn't have any of these. It is due to the internal witness of the Holy Spirit in his heart. He knows that material goods, health, and even fame will end when he moves on to the next chapter in glory in heaven, in eternal company with Jesus Christ. However, nothing and nobody can take away his confidence that he is full of the Holy Spirit and that God has transformed him completely, from the inside out.

Paul's mission is to be a magnifying glass of Christ. Christ the treasure, dwelling in the clay jar called Paul, is to shine through his life and his body. The afflictions, insults, struggles, rejection, and betrayals Paul suffers make the jar more transparent each time, making the Christ-treasure more evident and obvious in every action of his life. Truly, "whether by life or by death," Christ is always exalted in Paul's body.

Scriptural Context

Because the Sovereign LORD helps me, I will not be disgraced. Therefore have I set my face like flint, and I know I will not be put to shame. He who vindicates me is near. Who then will bring charges against me? Let us face each other! Who is my accuser? Let him confront me! It is the Sovereign LORD who helps me. Who will condemn me? They will all wear out like a garment; the moths will eat them up. (Isaiah 50:7–9)

The Spirit himself testifies with our spirit that we are God's children. (Romans 8:16)

But thanks be to God, who always leads us as captives in Christ's triumphal procession and uses us to spread the aroma of the knowledge of him everywhere. (2 Corinthians 2:14)

However, if you suffer as a Christian, do not be ashamed, but praise God that you bear that name. (1 Peter 4:16)

For Further Study
Psalm 62:5–8
Proverbs 10:28–30
2 Corinthians 4:7–10

Journal

Whom do you magnify? Make a list of all the actions, conversations, intentions, and encounters you had yesterday. Beside each action, place one, two, or three plus signs (+) depending on how much you magnified Christ. If you had harsh responses, unethical actions, or issues in which you did not give your all, place a minus sign (-) as an indication that you did not magnify Christ in your life. Ask God for forgiveness for such actions, and if God guides you to ask for forgiveness from the person you offended or harmed, obey! Also, give thanks for the ways in which God helped you magnify Christ in your life. Practice this spiritual discipline, and you will see how your life can become a light in the midst of a generation that walks in darkness.

_____

_____

_____

_____

_____

_____

_____

_____

_____

_____

_____

_____

_____

_____

_____

_____

_____

_____

_____

_____

_____

_____

_____

_____

PRAYER

Lord, give us the transparency that comes from radically obeying your will, your whisper in our lives, correcting our ways of being, our character, our vocabulary, our reactions. Continue to work in us until Christ can be seen through our lives in every circumstance.

27
ONLY ONE FOCUS

SCRIPTURE
Philippians 1:21

DEVOTIONAL REFLECTION
Paul has one focus, and that is Christ. All the aspects of his life are geared around Christ. His motivation, his efforts, his words, and his ministry are all centered on Christ. When we do not make Christ the center, things begin to fail.

Paul changed in a radical manner for Christ. He knows who he was before knowing Christ personally. But now he has been saturated internally by Christ. Every emotion, every fiber of his being, is full of the Holy Spirit. Everything that flows out of him is Christ. Christ in Paul is a river of living water that satisfies and nourishes not only his soul but also the souls and lives of those who are in contact with him as well.

If the Holy Spirit fills us, Christ is our passion, and God constantly receives glory through what we are and what we do. If the Holy Spirit fills us, we only have one goal, only one focus—to glorify God and demonstrate Christ 24 hours a day, 365 days a year. If the Holy Spirit fills us, Christ is the only motivation of our lives. It is a motivation that satisfies, does not disappoint, and gives fullness and satisfaction.

SCRIPTURAL CONTEXT
Jesus answered, "I am the way and the truth and the life. No one comes to the Father except through me." (John 14:6)

But these are written that you may believe that Jesus is the Messiah, the Son of God, and that by believing you may have life in his name. (John 20:31)

For in Christ all the fullness of the Deity lives in bodily form, and in Christ you have been brought to fullness. He is the head over every power and authority. (Colossians 2:9–10)

For Further Study
John 7:38
John 17:3
1 Corinthians 1:30–31
Galatians 2:20
Galatians 6:14

JOURNAL

Express in your own words what Paul means by his words in Philippians 1:21. In what concrete aspects of your life today can you apply this verse?

_____

_____

_____

_____

_____

_____

_____

_____

_____

_____

_____

_____

PRAYER

Let us pray with Peter, "Lord, to whom shall we go? You have the words of eternal life. We have come to believe and to know that you are the Holy One of God"(John 6:68–69).

28

THE GREATEST DILEMMA

SCRIPTURE
Philippians 1:21–24

DEVOTIONAL REFLECTION
It is evident that Paul has suffered a lot—persecution, scourging, sickness, prison, unfair jealousy, and underestimation of his authority and his ministry. Paul talks about having the desire to be with Jesus, which he understandably considers "better by far" than the circumstances he is going through. Yet Paul is "torn between the two." The coming glory is much more appealing than the present suffering.

Paul makes the decision of love—the decision to go on living and preaching and bringing more disciples into the body of Christ. His heart has been cleansed from any selfish desire, and he has surrendered completely to the will of God, to the calling God has given him. Paul's focus is double—to fulfill the will of God, the calling he has received, and to serve others with the love of Christ.

In spite of all the tribulations, temptations, and human weaknesses, God's calling keeps him anchored to the will of God. Even though he is experiencing a great dilemma, his love for God and for others solves the problem. Paul lives the greatest commandment to love God with all his heart, soul, mind, and strength.

SCRIPTURAL CONTEXT
The sting of death is sin, and the power of sin is the law. But thanks be to God! He gives us the victory through our Lord Jesus Christ. (1 Corinthians 15:56–57)

For though we live in the world, we do not wage war as the world does. The weapons we fight with are not the weapons of the world. On the contrary, they have divine power to demolish strongholds. We demolish arguments and every pretension that sets itself up against the knowledge of God, and we take captive every thought to make it obedient to Christ. And we will be ready to punish every act of disobedience, once your obedience is complete. (2 Corinthians 10:3–6)

For Further Study
Acts 26:15–19
Romans 8:35–37
2 Corinthians 5:1–5

JOURNAL

We all have dilemmas in our Christian lives. A dilemma is when there are two important options, and both cannot be fulfilled at the same time. We have to choose one or the other.

In the following lines, write about a dilemma related to spiritual affairs that you are experiencing. Explain what option you think you will choose. Write down a brief prayer asking God to help you understand his good and pleasing will.

_____

_____

_____

_____

_____

_____

_____

_____

_____

PRAYER

Let us pray with the apostle John: "Amen; come, Lord Jesus, come" (Maranatha). Lord, increase our desire to witness for Christ with our whole being, as long as God keeps us alive and as we wait for your second coming.

29 ❧
In Christ Hope Is Not Lost

Scripture
Philippians 1:25–26

Devotional Reflection
The phrase "convinced of this" can be translated, "I am completely persuaded." Paul's confidence is not human; it is supernatural. His confidence gives him hope. Even in prison, Paul has the hope of being helpful in the "progress and joy in the faith" of the Philippians. He dreams of seeing his beloved church that has supported him financially in his ministry.

The key of Paul's "supernatural" life is based on the fact that "God's love has been poured out into our hearts through the Holy Spirit." The key is the life of God *in* the Spirit, flowing through us to others. Paul's tribulations help him refine his patience, and his patience gives birth to hope. This type of "supernatural" life is available for all who want to live in Christ and by the Spirit as the base of their existence.

Scriptural Context
Not only so, but we also glory in our sufferings, because we know that suffering produces perseverance; perseverance, character; and character, hope. And hope does not put us to shame, because God's love has been poured out into our hearts through the Holy Spirit, who has been given to us. (Romans 5:3–5)

Now I rejoice in what I am suffering for you, and I fill up in my flesh what is still lacking in regard to Christ's afflictions, for the sake of his body, which is the church. I have become its servant by the commission God gave me to present to you the word of God in its fullness. (Colossians 1:24–25)

For Further Study
Acts 20:25–28
Romans 15:28–29
Philemon 1:22

JOURNAL

Define what it means for the believer and disciple of Christ to have a supernatural life. Give some examples, as a testimony, of supernatural circumstances in your own life.

_____

_____

_____

_____

_____

_____

_____

_____

_____

_____

_____

_____

_____

_____

_____

PRAYER

Let us pray with Paul, "May the God of hope fill you with all joy and peace as you trust in him, so that you may overflow with hope by the power of the Holy Spirit" (Romans 15:13).

30

FIRM AND IN ONE SPIRIT

SCRIPTURE
Philippians 1:27–28

DEVOTIONAL REFLECTION
Paul exhorts the Philippians to behave themselves, that their conduct and conversation be worthy of the gospel of Christ. The church needs the same message. Behaving as worthy of the gospel of Christ means 1) to be firm in one Spirit; 2) to strive together as one; and 3) to not be frightened by those who oppose us.

This is the first time in the epistle that Paul talks about being in one Spirit and as one for the faith. If we examine the whole letter, we find that this is the central theme. The unity of the members of the church must be based on the unity that each person must have in having the same mindset as Christ. If each person is in intimate union with Jesus, they have the same purpose and mind as him. Therefore, there will automatically be unity in the church.

In spite of the differences each one has, they can persevere in unity. That kind of unity brings growth.

SCRIPTURAL CONTEXT
As a prisoner for the Lord, then, I urge you to live a life worthy of the calling you have received. Be completely humble and gentle; be patient, bearing with one another in love. Make every effort to keep the unity of the Spirit through the bond of peace. There is one body and one Spirit, just as you were called to one hope when you were called; one Lord, one faith, one baptism, one God and Father of all, who is over all and through all and in all. (Ephesians 4:1–6)

For Further Study
Romans 1:16
Philippians 2:5
1 Thessalonians 2:11–12
1 Thessalonians 4:1–3

JOURNAL

What does "as one for the faith" mean to you? In what way does the unity of Jesus with his Father and the Holy Spirit explain the expression "as one for the faith"?

_____

_____

_____

_____

_____

_____

_____

_____

_____

_____

_____

_____

_____

_____

_____

_____

PRAYER

Lord, help us to find our unity in you, showing your character through our behavior, our words, and our lives.

31
CHRISTIAN PERSPECTIVE ON SUFFERING

SCRIPTURE
Philippians 1:29–30

DEVOTIONAL REFLECTION

Christians are not masochists; that is, we do not have fun suffering, nor do we seek to suffer. On the contrary, being a Christian is having life in abundance in the Lord Jesus Christ. God grants us amazing blessings that are in store for us in the Word of God, and that become a reality as we serve him. However, deciding to be godly people (true worshipers; see John 4:22–24) will launch us offensively toward the powers of Satan, which will attack us back. Really, it is not something personal toward us, but an attack to the body of Christ—his bride, his church.

Nevertheless, the picture is not entirely negative. Jesus encourages us in John 16:33 by assuring us that he has already "overcome the world." Anyone who does not present this aspect of the Christian life and deceives new followers and disciples of Christ, telling them there is no suffering in being a Christian, is a liar and a false prophet.

There are four different possible causes of suffering. The first is due to being part of the world, which is under the curse. Suffering in the world is inevitable. We pray not to suffer and not to experience this type of suffering. We ourselves participate in environmental destruction, we can catch a virus or illness, sometimes we find ourselves the victims of natural disasters or pure accidents, our bodies deteriorate, and we suffer the consequences of the fall and the curse of creation (see Genesis 3:17). Still, God offers the hope of redemption from this kind of suffering (see Romans 8:20–23).

The second type of suffering is due to committed sins. Each sin brings its own consequences. The sad thing is that not only do we ourselves suffer for the sins we've committed, but we also make others suffer because of our sins, and the consequences of our sins can harm many people.

Third, we suffer as we live holy and godly lives. Our lives become agents of conviction for others. We are the light and salt of the earth, and people will react negatively toward the kingdom. These reactions can harm us physically and emotionally (sometimes those closest to us harm us the most).

The fourth type of suffering is the pain of seeing so many people headed toward destruction. This is the labor pain that Christians feel. We identify with the pain of Christ for the lost, and we are willing to do whatever is necessary to reach others for Christ. As Christians we say, "Your will be done!" no matter what happens.

The key to all of this is to know what to do with suffering. If we know it is inevitable, we can use it to build our life and strengthen ourselves in the Lord.

Scriptural Context

Blessed are those who are persecuted because of righteousness, for theirs is the kingdom of heaven. Blessed are you when people insult you, persecute you and falsely say all kinds of evil against you because of me. Rejoice and be glad, because great is your reward in heaven, for in the same way they persecuted the prophets who were before you. (Matthew 5:10–12)

I have told you these things, so that in me you may have peace. In this world you will have trouble. But take heart! I have overcome the world. (John 16:33)

Now I rejoice in what I am suffering for you, and I fill up in my flesh what is still lacking in regard to Christ's afflictions, for the sake of his body, which is the church. (Colossians 1:24)

When tempted, no one should say, "God is tempting me." For God cannot be tempted by evil, nor does he tempt anyone. (James 1:13)

For Further Study
Job 1:1–12
Acts 4:40–42
Romans 5:3–5
2 Timothy 3:11–12
James 1:17
1 Peter 4:13–14

JOURNAL

List the four types of suffering and give some personal examples of each one in your life. Select one of the passages from the Scriptural Context section and dedicate some time to meditating on it and applying it to your situation.

_____

_____

_____

_____

_____

_____

_____

_____

_____

_____

_____

_____

_____

PRAYER

Lord, help us to use our suffering for your glory and honor. Protect us from the Evil One and from temptations. Strengthen us through your Holy Spirit in the midst of trials and suffering.

UNIT 2
THE MIND OF CHRIST,
THE MODEL FOR CHRISTIANS

32

Request for Disciples Who Follow Christ

Scripture

Philippians 2:1–2

Devotional Reflection

Studying chapter 2 of the letter to the Philippians is like entering the Holy of Holies, to the very presence of God, especially in 2:5–10. Think for a moment on what this means. Paul begins with an interjection that indicates consequence: *Therefore.* This introduction connects us with Philippians 1:20–25, where Paul talks about his calling and the decisions he has made.

Paul asks the Philippians to make his joy complete. He urges them to be like Jesus. He wants them to be like his Hero, his Savior, his Sanctifier, his Counselor, his Lord Jesus Christ. The phrase "being like-minded, having the same love, being one in spirit and of one mind" seems to be a series of redundancies, but it is a hyperbole that points to verses 5 through 11 of chapter 2. This phrase is a calling to unity in and with Christ. It is a commentary and an application of the priestly prayer of Jesus documented in John 17. The author of Hebrews does exactly the same thing in Hebrews 12:2, and Paul does it again in Colossians 3:1–3.

Victory in the Christian life comes when we focus on the person of Christ, keeping everything that he has commanded us, allowing Jesus to be the way, the truth and the life.

Scriptural Context

That all of them may be one, Father, just as you are in me and I am in you. May they also be in us so that the world may believe that you have sent me. I have given them the glory that you gave me, that they may be one as we are one—I in them and you in me—so that they may be brought to complete unity. Then the world will know that you sent me and have loved them even as you have loved me. (John 17:21–23)

Live in harmony with one another. Do not be proud, but be willing to associate with people of low position. Do not be conceited. Do not repay anyone evil for evil. Be careful to do what is right in the eyes of everyone. If it is possible, as far as it depends on you, live at peace with everyone. (Romans 12:16–18)

For Further Study
Matthew 11:25–30
1 Corinthians 11:1
Ephesians 4:3–6

JOURNAL

For a moment, pretend that this letter is not addressed to the Philippians but to you. Do you realize that you have a huge challenge to fulfill? To be like Jesus! On your own, briefly describe what it means for you to be like Christ. Make a list of ten qualities that you need to cultivate in order to be more like Jesus.

_____

_____

_____

_____

_____

_____

_____

_____

_____

_____

_____

_____

_____

_____

_____

_____

_____

_____

_____

_____

_____

_____

_____

_____

_____

_____

_____

_____

_____

_____

_____

_____

_____

PRAYER

Father, thank you for offering Jesus to give us life. Thank you for allowing the Holy Spirit to come into our lives to help us focus on Jesus, our Savior and Sanctifier. Thank you for giving us the example of the greatest, extravagant, and incomparable love. Live that love through us.

33
AN ATTITUDE THAT HINDERS US

SCRIPTURE
Philippians 2:3–4

DEVOTIONAL REFLECTION
There is nothing that can stop the grace and powerful moving of God more than ambition, vain conceit, fleshly pride and selfishness—that search for self-exaltation and self-fulfillment. People who are vain, proud, ambitious, selfish, and centered on themselves are preoccupied with achievements, material things, titles, and positions. These types of people are an X-ray of Satan's philosophy.

Unfortunately, we are all born with carnal egoism. Theologians define this fleshly selfishness as original sin, or innate depravity. The original sin with which we are born is the source of our sinful thoughts and actions. Jesus died on the cross to cleanse us from such pollution, from that nature.

Paul, in these verses, explains what the opposite of vanity, fleshly selfishness, and arrogant pride is. The supreme example of the emptying of self is the Lord Jesus Christ, whom Paul describes in Philippians 2:5–11. The only one who can cleanse a person of vanity, fleshly selfishness, arrogant pride, and the search for selfish benefits and self-exaltation is the Holy Spirit in his sanctifying power.

Christian holiness is more than a pious morality, following certain rules and legalism, or appearing to be godly. Holiness is the cleansing and purification of the heart.

On the day of Pentecost, the disciples and all the others present are cleansed from fleshly selfishness, self-seeking, self-fulfillment, and self-promotion (Acts 15:8–9). Now they are not filled with themselves but are full of the almighty God, filled with the mind of Christ.

Scriptural Context

The LORD saw how great the wickedness of the human race had become on the earth, and that every inclination of the thoughts of the human heart was only evil all the time. (Genesis 6:5)

The heart is deceitful above all things and beyond cure. Who can understand it? (Jeremiah 17:9)

For out of the heart come evil thoughts—murder, adultery, sexual immorality, theft, false testimony, slander. (Matthew 15:19)

But if you harbor bitter envy and selfish ambition in your hearts, do not boast about it or deny the truth. Such "wisdom" does not come down from heaven but is earthly, unspiritual, demonic. For where you have envy and selfish ambition, there you find disorder and every evil practice. (James 3:14–16)

For Further Study
Acts 20:19
2 Corinthians 11:14–15
Galatians 5:26
1 Peter 5:5–6
1 Peter 3:8–12
1 John 1:9

Journal

Think of your own life X-ray—not taken by a doctor but by the Holy Spirit. Write down what you see and the solution that this chapter presents for the purity and cleansing of the heart.

_____

_____

_____

_____

_____

_____

_____

_____

_____

_____

_____

_____

_____

_____

_____

_____

_____

_____

_____

_____

_____

PRAYER

Test me, Lord, and try me. Examine my heart and my mind (Psalm 26:2); search me, God, and know my heart; test me and know my anxious thoughts. See if there is any offensive way in me, and lead me in the way everlasting (Psalm 139:23–24); wash away all my iniquity and cleanse me from my sin (Psalm 51:2).

34

FULL CONCENTRATION

SCRIPTURE
Philippians 2:5

DEVOTIONAL REFLECTION

The word "mindset" in Greek is *proneo*. The New Testament definition of this word is "to exercise the mind—that is, to have an opinion, a sentiment, or passion, and by implication, being mentally willing, or intensely interested in something that has to be obeyed" (Strong's Dictionary). Philippians 2:5 is the introduction of the passage called *kenosis*, which means to empty oneself, to let everything go completely. Paul is inviting the Philippians to have the same mental disposition, strength, and passion that Jesus Christ had to obediently fulfill the mission the Father gave him. He accepted it with all his being and strength, without minding the cost of fulfilling such a mission.

To be a disciple, a follower of Christ, is to adopt his way of thinking and feeling. It is being willing to adopt his mission with everything it might entail. The key is to deny ourselves and take up our crosses daily and follow him. Following him is to focus on Jesus and follow him where he went, to the cross, to give his life for me and for all of humanity. It is more than the emotional moment of going to an altar and consecrating our lives to him. It is a mental disposition; it is every day, every moment. It is a focus on doing only the will of God.

On occasion, we think that not doing the will of God means to commit extreme sins, like killing, robbing a bank, and so on. But it is not like that. You and I stop doing the will of God when we don't consider the person who is suffering, the one who needs forgiveness, when we harm others with our words, when we do not know how to keep quiet and hug the one who is in need.

Scriptural Context

Then he said to them all: "Whoever wants to be my disciple must deny themselves and take up their cross daily and follow me. For whoever wants to save their life will lose it, but whoever loses their life for me will save it." (Luke 9:23–24)

To this you were called, because Christ suffered for you, leaving you an example, that you should follow in his steps. "He committed no sin, and no deceit was found in his mouth." When they hurled their insults at him, he did not retaliate; when he suffered, he made no threats. Instead, he entrusted himself to him who judges justly. "He himself bore our sins" in his body on the cross, so that we might die to sins and live for righteousness; "by his wounds you have been healed." (1 Peter 2:21–24)

For Further Study
John 4:34
John 6:38
Romans 15:3
Ephesians 5:2

Journal

Have you emptied yourself to make room for Jesus in your heart? Are there moments in which you stop doing the will of God and are guided by your own thinking? How can you deny yourself in your home, in your place of work, with your friends, in the local church? Write down some of your thoughts.

_____

_____

_____

_____

_____

_____

_____

_____

_____

_____

_____

_____

_____

_____

_____

_____

_____

_____

_____

_____

_____

_____

_____

_____

_____

_____

_____

_____

PRAYER

Lord, prosper us in love! Fill us until we overflow with your love to give it out to a world that desperately seeks love—real love, unconditional love, love that suffers, your love. Help us pour out our lives of love to others, to present your love through our attitudes, our actions, our words, and our deeds. Open our eyes to see the needs of others and allow us to love them with your love.

35

POSITION OR RANK?

SCRIPTURE
Philippians 2:5–6

DEVOTIONAL REFLECTION

The apostle Paul invites the Philippians to have the same way of thinking, feeling, and acting as that of Christ. He invites them to take the steps that Jesus took to fulfill the will of his Father in obedience. The first step Jesus took was that he "did not consider equality with God something to be used to his own advantage." Jesus is God, completely God—"being in very nature God."

The expression "did not consider" does not mean he did not value being equal to God. *Consider* can also be translated *regard*—that is, he considered carefully his position and rank; he thought in a meticulous way about what he needed to do to fulfill God's commission.

This first step is mental; it is a consideration. Jesus, in his mind, made a decision of not being equal to God. This does not mean that he stopped *being* God. It means he lowered his rank and position in order to depend completely on God.

If we want to be true disciples, following Jesus will cost us everything we have.

SCRIPTURAL CONTEXT

In the beginning was the Word, and the Word was with God, and the Word was God. (John 1:1)

For this reason they tried all the more to kill him; not only was he breaking the Sabbath, but he was even calling God his own Father, making himself equal with God. (John 5:18)

I and the Father are one. (John 10:30)

Therefore, I urge you, brothers and sisters, in view of God's mercy, to offer your bodies as a living sacrifice, holy and pleasing to God—this is your true and proper worship. Do not conform to the pattern of this world, but be transformed by the renewing of your mind. Then you will be able to test and approve what God's will is—his good, pleasing and perfect will. (Romans 12:1–2)

The Son is the image of the invisible God, the firstborn over all creation. (Colossians 1:15)

For Further Study
Luke 14:27–30
John 20:28
Hebrews 1:2–3

JOURNAL

Based on Romans 12:2 and Jesus's decision not to consider equality with God something to be used to his own advantage, what do you think it means to be transformed by the renewing of your mind? Write down specifically how you can have the mind of Christ, how you can take the first step to understand the position or rank you have, and how you can give it up.

_____

_____

_____

_____

_____

_____

_____

_____

_____

_____

_____

_____

_____

_____

_____

_____

_____

_____

_____

_____

_____

_____

_____

_____

_____

_____

_____

_____

_____

_____

PRAYER

Lord, open up our minds so we can consider the cost of discipleship—to consider what it means to embrace your mission, your way of thinking, and your way of feeling. Help us to be obedient after considering all this.

36

JESUS DID NOT CLING TO HIS POSITION

SCRIPTURE
Philippians 2:6

DEVOTIONAL REFLECTION

Something typical of all people is to get attached to material things, titles, achievements, and loved ones. Because of our fallen nature, we are born with closed fists until God shows us through Jesus Christ what it means to be real people. As we see our Savior die on a cross with open arms, we see that he was not attached to anything of this world!

The expression "to be used to his own advantage" comes from a root that means steal, take forcefully, or snatch. This is the only time it is mentioned in the New Testament. Jesus did not hold on to being like his Father.

The first step Jesus took to fulfill the mission God gave him was to leave his rank and position—an act of his mind. The second step was the concrete action of opening his hands and not holding on to anything: He kept his hands open his whole life. And he still has them open!

SCRIPTURAL CONTEXT

But when the set time had fully come, God sent his Son, born of a woman, born under the law, to redeem those under the law, that we might receive adoption to sonship. (Galatians 4:4–5)

Beyond all question, the mystery from which true godliness springs is great: He appeared in the flesh, was vindicated by the Spirit, was seen by angels, was preached among the nations, was believed on in the world, was taken up in glory. (1 Timothy 3:16)

But we do see Jesus, who was made lower than the angels for a little while, now crowned with glory and honor because he suffered death, so that by the grace of God he might taste death for everyone. In bringing many sons and daughters to glory, it was fitting that God, for whom and through whom everything exists, should make the pioneer of their salvation perfect through what he suffered. (Hebrews 2:9–10)

Jesus Christ is the same yesterday and today and forever. (Hebrews 13:8)

For Further Study
Isaiah 9:6
Matthew 6:31–33
1 Corinthians 15:45–49

JOURNAL

Write a list of things you are holding on to, whether material, emotional, or mental. What would happen if you did not have these things? Express your thoughts in the following lines.

_____

_____

_____

_____

_____

_____

_____

_____

_____

_____

PRAYER

Lord, we offer you our clean hands that do not hold on to anything except you. We seek your kingdom with a pure heart that is filled with your presence.

37

HE MADE HIMSELF NOTHING

SCRIPTURE
Philippians 2:7

DEVOTIONAL REFLECTION

The expression "made himself nothing" is *ekenosen* in Greek; it means complete emptying, not leaving anything for oneself. Jesus, temporarily, put aside all the attributes of being God, except that of being a God of love and holiness. He did not *stop* being God. He simply limited himself by not using everything that belonged to him *as* God.

Jesus was also completely human at the same time as he was completely God. This paradox is a mystery that is impossible to explain in our human minds. He, as a person, was just like a Christian filled with the Holy Spirit. An in-depth study of the temptations shows Jesus depending on the Word of God, on prayer, and on the power of the Holy Spirit to destroy Satan. He did not use his resources as God; he abstained from doing so. He came to be the second Adam, to show us how a person can live 100 percent dedicated to fulfill the will of God, depending completely on God for everything, and also to show us how a person can live in holiness and in victory over sin.

Jesus's emptying benefits us in at least three different ways: a) He overcame sin in his body and defeated the armies of darkness; b) he offered himself as the perfect Lamb, pure and without blemish, as the holy person to pay for our sins; c) he opened the door for us to receive the Holy Spirit as purifying fire, as power over temptation and sin, and as power to be his witnesses. All of these benefits for us cost everything of Jesus, absolutely everything!

We empty ourselves completely to be fully filled with God.

Scriptural Context

Rejoice greatly, Daughter Zion! Shout, Daughter Jerusalem! See, your king comes to you, righteous and victorious, lowly and riding on a donkey, on a colt, the foal of a donkey. (Zechariah 9:9)

About three in the afternoon Jesus cried out in a loud voice, "Eli, Eli, lema sabachthani?" (which means "My God, my God, why have you forsaken me?"). (Matthew 27:46)

For this reason he had to be made like them, fully human in every way, in order that he might become a merciful and faithful high priest in service to God, and that he might make atonement for the sins of the people. Because he himself suffered when he was tempted, he is able to help those who are being tempted. (Hebrews 2:17–18)

For we do not have a high priest who is unable to empathize with our weaknesses, but we have one who has been tempted in every way, just as we are—yet he did not sin. Let us then approach God's throne of grace with confidence, so that we may receive mercy and find grace to help us in our time of need. (Hebrews 4:15–16)

For Further Study
Matthew 13:55–57
John 1:14
Romans 15:3
Romans 15:8

Journal

Pray about whatever it is that controls you or does not allow you to depend on God. Write it down in the following lines. Then pray and ask God to fill you with the fullness of the Holy Spirit.

_____

_____

_____

_____

_____

_____

_____

_____

_____

_____

_____

_____

_____

_____

_____

_____

_____

_____

_____

_____

_____

_____

_____

_____

_____

_____

PRAYER

Lord, today I give up everything that controls me. I empty myself completely, following your example. I ask for your infilling. Fill me today!

38 ❧
COMPLETE HUMILITY

SCRIPTURE
Philippians 2:7

DEVOTIONAL REFLECTION

There is a contrast between verses 6 and 7 in Philippians 2: "being in very nature God" and "taking the very nature of a servant." This is another step in the ladder of success for the fulfillment of the mission of the Father! In this case, each step goes lower, as opposed to the success of the world, where the purpose is always to go higher and increase in power. This step down is an abysmal step—from God to slave. The Message translation presents this contrast in a clearer form: "When the time came, he set aside the privileges of deity and took on the status of a slave, became *human*!"

In the Old Testament, two types of slaves are mentioned—the slave who was bought and served out of fear of being punished and the slave who served out of love for his master and decided to serve his master his whole life. Jesus Christ, being God, made himself a slave out of love for his Father, in order to fulfill the most important mission of all ages—a mission that has eternal consequences for all of us.

Paul continues to present all the steps Jesus took to fulfill his mission with success: a) He didn't consider his position or rank; b) he didn't hold on to anything; c) he emptied himself completely and made himself nothing; d) and now he humbles himself no matter the consequences, emptying himself of his attributes as God, coming to us as a slave for love of the Father and love for us.

Paul invites us to have the same attitude, the same mind as Christ. It is the only way of fulfilling the Great Commission, to be like him!

Scriptural Context

After he has suffered, he will see the light of life and be satisfied; by his knowledge my righteous servant will justify many, and he will bear their iniquities. (Isaiah 53:11)

When he had finished washing their feet, he put on his clothes and returned to his place. "Do you understand what I have done for you?" he asked them. "You call me 'Teacher' and 'Lord,' and rightly so, for that is what I am. Now that I, your Lord and Teacher, have washed your feet, you also should wash one another's feet." (John 13:12–14)

For you know the grace of our Lord Jesus Christ, that though he was rich, yet for your sake he became poor, so that you through his poverty might become rich. (2 Corinthians 8:9)

For Further Study
Matthew 11:28–30
Matthew 20:26–28
Romans 8:3

Journal

Define what it means to be a slave and for how long one has to serve. Then think about the service that Jesus has offered you. Write about it in the following lines.

_____

_____

_____

_____

_____

_____

_____

_____

_____

_____

_____

_____

_____

_____

_____

_____

_____

_____

_____

_____

_____

_____

_____

_____

_____

_____

_____

_____

_____

PRAYER

Holy Father, thank you for sending your Son to serve us with his own life. What a sacrifice! What an honor! Help us do the same for you out of love.

39

FULL IDENTIFICATION WITH HUMANITY

SCRIPTURE
Philippians 2:6–7

DEVOTIONAL REFLECTION

The fact that the Son of God made himself in human likeness is a great mystery. Hundreds of books have been written about this, and still today it is hard to understand the depth of this fact. Just like Moses in the desert, as we face this historical fact, we find ourselves on holy ground, and there is nothing we can do except humble ourselves as we witness such amazing love—God seeking us at our own level, communicating in the same way we do.

The Bible is clear in that Jesus, being God, was also completely human. Jesus was hungry, Jesus cried, Jesus suffered pain, Jesus was tempted in everything just like us—but he never sinned. Even though he was human in everything, in his humanity Jesus defeated sin, defeated death, and he is our Deliverer (the Christ, the Messiah).

Jesus has authority. In the beginning it was an authority received from the Father. However, Jesus ratified his authority by being radically obedient to the Father's will. Jesus is our greatest example, and being completely human, he reclaimed the human race.

Jesus identifies completely with you and me.

REFLECTIONS

Therefore the Lord himself will give you a sign: The virgin will conceive and give birth to a son, and will call him Immanuel. (Isaiah 7:14)

Then Jesus came to them and said, "All authority in heaven and on earth has been given to me." (Matthew 28:18)

The people were amazed at his teaching, because he taught them as one who had authority, not as the teachers of the law. (Mark 1:22)

Therefore let all Israel be assured of this: God has made this Jesus, whom you crucified, both Lord and Messiah. (Acts 2:36)

Son though he was, he learned obedience from what he suffered and, once made perfect, he became the source of eternal salvation for all who obey him. (Hebrews 5:8–9)

For Further Study
Isaiah 9:6
Matthew 1:23–25
Luke 1:74–75
Luke 2:10–12
1 Timothy 2:5
Hebrews 4:15–16

JOURNAL

Write down in what ways Jesus identifies himself with you.

_____

_____

_____

_____

_____

_____

_____

_____

_____

_____

_____

_____

_____

_____

_____

_____

_____

_____

_____

_____

_____

_____

_____

_____

_____

_____

_____

_____

_____

_____

_____

_____

PRAYER

Eternal Father, thank you for sending your Son to be exactly like us, human with the same characteristics as all of us. Thank you for sending an example of what you had in mind for our lives. Thank you for sending us a Conqueror and Deliverer. Thank you for opening a door for us to have a victorious life and complete joy through Jesus Christ.

40
He Humbled Himself

Scripture
Philippians 2:8

Devotional Reflection
Jesus continues to climb down the ladder in order to fulfill his purpose and mission.

1) He didn't consider his position or rank.
2) He didn't hold on to his attributes as God.
3) He emptied himself completely and made himself nothing.
4) He made himself our slave.
5) He made himself human, exactly like us—but without sin.
6) And now he humbles himself.

Humbling oneself does not mean servility. "He humbled himself" means he begged God with anguish for another option to fulfill his mission. Jesus's humbling is an act of desperation, thinking he would have to separate himself from the Father. How could he go through such suffering?

At one point or another in our lives, God will ask for something we do not understand, and we will try to beg to be spared that cup. Just like Jesus, we can go to him, humble ourselves, and ask him to consider another plan of action. Coming to God in that way is not arrogance or disobedience. It is a way to make sure that the step we are about to take is really the will of God.

Scriptural Context
My sacrifice, O God, is a broken spirit; a broken and contrite heart you, God, will not despise. (Psalm 51:17)

Wisdom's instruction is to fear the LORD, and humility comes before honor. (Proverbs 15:33)

Going a little farther, he fell with his face to the ground and prayed, "My Father, if it is possible, may this cup be taken from me. Yet not as I will, but as you will." (Matthew 26:39)

For just as through the disobedience of the one man the many were made sinners, so also through the obedience of the one man the many will be made righteous. (Romans 5:19)

For Further Study
Philippians 3:21
Hebrews 10:5–10

JOURNAL

Define what it means to humble oneself according to what you read in the Scriptural Context section. Write about a situation that requires you to kneel down before God, and pray in the way Jesus did.

_____

_____

_____

_____

_____

_____

_____

_____

_____

_____

_____

PRAYER

Holy Father, we come to you to ask for wisdom to face this day. Keep us from the Evil One and help us do your will, although we might not understand what that means.

41
DEATH ON A CROSS

SCRIPTURE
Philippians 2:8

DEVOTIONAL REFLECTION
The values of the kingdom of God are completely opposite to the values of the world. The world wants to live by the sacrifice of others. The kingdom gives everything without considering the cost. Jesus makes the greatest demonstration of not holding on by opening his arms and giving his life for us. The greatest step to success in the kingdom is to be willing to give your life for others out of unconditional love.

Being friends of Jesus is the greatest privilege we could have. Above all, he is a friend we can trust in, and we can talk to him every day.

Jesus desired just one thing—to do the will of the Father. It cost him everything, even his very life. To do the will of God, there is only one condition: Give up everything; desire nothing except God, which means to do his will.

Purity of heart only happens when there is complete consecration. Jesus doesn't require from us anything that he hasn't already done.

SCRIPTURAL CONTEXT
Dogs surround me, a pack of villains encircles me; they pierce my hands and my feet. All my bones are on display; people stare and gloat over me. They divide my clothes among them and cast lots for my garment. (Psalm 22:16–18)

Blessed are the pure in heart, for they will see God. (Matthew 5:8)

Therefore, I urge you, brothers and sisters, in view of God's mercy, to offer your bodies as a living sacrifice, holy and pleasing to God—this is your true and proper worship. Do not conform to the pattern of this world, but be transformed by the renewing of your mind. Then you will be able to test and approve what God's will is—his good, pleasing and perfect will. (Romans 12:1–2)

For Further Study
John 10:17–18
John 15:13–14
John 17:17
John 17:19
Galatians 3:13–14
Philippians 2:21
1 Peter 2:21–24
1 Peter 3:18

JOURNAL

Make a list of the good things you think you could never leave to do the will of God. In a consecration prayer, give them to God, and allow him to take control over all those things.

_____

_____

_____

_____

_____

_____

_____

_____

_____

_____

PRAYER

Lord, teach us to know you more; help us to live the values of the kingdom, helping us focus on doing your will.

42

CONSEQUENCES OF DOING THE WILL OF GOD

SCRIPTURE
Philippians 2:9

DEVOTIONAL REFLECTION

Jesus, out of love for the Father, gave everything to fulfill his will. He did everything with excellence and radical obedience. "Therefore" refers to the consequence of doing something. Paul says that, because Jesus acted according to the will of God, his Father "exalted him to the highest place."

Jesus did not expect a reward for doing the will of God in a radical and excellent way. But the Father responds in grace and exalts him to the highest place. The expression "exalted him to the highest place" is only one word in the original language. Part of the word is *hupor*, from which the words *hyperbole* and *hyperactive* come. The word means the highest place, the highest position, the highest honor.

God's response to our consecration is to use us according to the desires of his will. The reward for our obedience is higher than heaven, more than honors or position; it is the satisfaction of being used by God in the best way possible.

SCRIPTURAL CONTEXT

God exalted him to his own right hand as Prince and Savior that he might bring Israel to repentance and forgive their sins. (Acts 5:31)

For this very reason, Christ died and returned to life so that he might be the Lord of both the dead and the living. (Romans 14:9)

For he "has put everything under his feet." Now when it says that "everything" has been put under him, it is clear that this does not include God himself, who put everything under Christ. When he has done this, then the Son himself will be made subject to him who put everything under him, so that God may be all in all. (1 Corinthians 15:27–28)

But we do see Jesus, who was made lower than the angels for a little while, now crowned with glory and honor because he suffered death, so that by the grace of God he might taste death for everyone. (Hebrews 2:9)

He received honor and glory from God the Father when the voice came to him from the Majestic Glory, saying, "This is my Son, whom I love; with him I am well pleased." (2 Peter 1:17)

JOURNAL

Write about one or two situations in which God has honored you more than what you deserve. Write about how that glorified God.

_____

_____

_____

_____

_____

_____

_____

_____

_____

_____

_____

PRAYER

Lord, help us to use suffering for your honor and glory. Protect us from the Evil One and temptations, and strengthen us through your Holy Spirit in the midst of trials and suffering.

43

THE HIGHEST NAME

SCRIPTURE
Philippians 2:10

DEVOTIONAL REFLECTION
"In a loud voice they were saying: 'Worthy is the Lamb, who was slain, to receive power and wealth and wisdom and strength and honor and glory and praise!' Then I heard every creature in heaven and on earth and under the earth and on the sea, and all that is in them, saying: 'To him who sits on the throne and to the Lamb be praise and honor and glory and power, for ever and ever!'" (Revelation 5:12–13).

Jesus is the sweetest name I can pronounce. Jesus is the hope that becomes a reality here on earth. Jesus is the Prince of shepherds, the great Shepherd of the sheep. He is the most tender and understanding person.

SCRIPTURAL CONTEXT
For to us a child is born, to us a son is given, and the government will be on his shoulders. And he will be called Wonderful Counselor, Mighty God, Everlasting Father, Prince of Peace. Of the greatness of his government and peace there will be no end. He will reign on David's throne and over his kingdom, establishing and upholding it with justice and righteousness from that time on and forever. The zeal of the LORD Almighty will accomplish this. (Isaiah 9:6–7)

Salvation is found in no one else, for there is no other name under heaven given to mankind by which we must be saved. (Acts 4:12)

Now to the King eternal, immortal, invisible, the only God, be honor and glory for ever and ever. Amen. (1 Timothy 1:17)

For Further Study
Psalm 72:11–13
Psalm 89:27
Isaiah 49:7
Ephesians 1:18–23
1 Timothy 1:17
1 Timothy 6:14–16
1 Peter 3:21–22
Revelation 19:13–16
Revelation 21:22–27

JOURNAL

After reading the verses listed in the Scriptural Context section, write down the answers to these questions: Who is Jesus? Who is Jesus *for you*?

_____

_____

_____

_____

_____

_____

_____

_____

_____

_____

_____

_____

_____

PRAYER

Jesus, thank you!

44

THE FRUIT OF LOVE AND RADICAL OBEDIENCE

SCRIPTURE

Philippians 2:10

DEVOTIONAL REFLECTION

The expression "that at" indicates consequence. Because of the steps Jesus took in order to do the will of God and to save us, every knee will bow, in heaven and on earth and under the earth. Bowing our knees means submission. On the day of the second coming of our Lord Jesus Christ, every living being will submit to him.

This does not happen today, for there are many who still do not recognize Jesus as the God Almighty, Creator and Sustainer of everything that exists. Many times, we think everyone knows Jesus, but there are countries in which the citizens have never heard about him or his redeeming work. However, one day faith will cease to exist (see 1 Corinthians 13:8–13), and everything will be obvious, and there will be no other option except to bow down in submission to Jesus, recognizing that he is the King of kings and the Lord of lords.

All of us who have accepted Jesus's sacrifice on the cross and his salvation bow before him today, and we praise him in submission out of love, not submission out of fear; it is a submission full of respect and reverence. We should be aware that bowing our knees before God is surrendering wholeheartedly to his lordship. The truth is that, if we give in to God, we give up other things, like sin.

SCRIPTURAL CONTEXT

You, then, why do you judge your brother or sister? Or why do you treat them with contempt? For we will all stand before God's judgment seat. It is written: "As surely as I live," says the Lord, "every knee will bow before me; every tongue will acknowledge God." (Romans 14:10–11)

Dear friends, now we are children of God, and what we will be has not yet been made known. But we know that when Christ appears, we shall be like him, for we shall see him as he is. All who have this hope in him purify themselves, just as he is pure. (1 John 3:2–3)

Then I heard every creature in heaven and on earth and under the earth and on the sea, and all that is in them, saying: "To him who sits on the throne and to the Lamb be praise and honor and glory and power, for ever and ever!" The four living creatures said, "Amen," and the elders fell down and worshiped. (Revelation 5:13–14)

For Further Study
Colossians 1:15–20
Revelation 6:12–17

JOURNAL

Who is your Lord? To whom do you surrender your will? Your lifestyle will reflect your answer to this question. Think about some spiritual disciplines that will help you recognize that Jesus is the owner and Lord of your life, and write them down.

_____

_____

_____

_____

_____

_____

_____

_____

_____

_____

_____

_____

_____

_____

_____

_____

_____

_____

_____

_____

_____

_____

_____

_____

_____

_____

_____

_____

_____

_____

_____

_____

_____

PRAYER

Lord, we recognize you as the only Lord of everything and of our own lives. We bow our knees before you as a sign of reverence, love, and submission.

45 ❧
CONFESSION

SCRIPTURE
Philippians 2:11

DEVOTIONAL REFLECTION

Jesus's choice to obey the will of God potentially assured the salvation of every person. That is, we are not saved until we decide to follow Jesus and accept the gift of his redeeming death on the cross. However, even though glorious salvation is available for everyone, one needs to choose to receive it through: 1) repentance; 2) confession of sins (sin that is not confessed is one of the greatest obstacles for a church to prosper; some people, instead of confessing their sins, hide them, but God cannot be hidden from); 3) receiving Christ in our hearts as Savior and Lord; 4) obeying the will of the Father, showing that he is really our Lord. Only those who follow these steps will enjoy an intimate relationship with Jesus, the Father, and the Holy Spirit from now until eternity, if they remain faithful and obedient until death or until Jesus's second coming.

We cannot receive the salvation Christ offers if we do not follow the steps of repentance, confession, receiving Christ, and obedience. However, there are people who voluntarily decide to continue their sinful lifestyles and reject the gift of salvation Jesus offers, and therefore, they are destined for eternal unhappiness and suffering. The consequences of a sinful life are inevitable. However, one day (at Jesus's second coming) those who have received him, as well as those who have rejected him, will bow their knees before Jesus and declare that he is the Lord of lords and the King of kings.

There is still one question to answer: What is the reason that at the name of Jesus every knee should bow, in heaven and on earth and under the earth, and every tongue acknowledge that Jesus Christ is

Lord? Philippians 2:11 answers that question: "to the glory of God the Father." Our Lord Jesus's obedience and sacrifice offered us present and eternal salvation, but he also worships, glorifies, and honors his Father. Ultimately, our reason for existing as a human race is to give glory and honor to God.

SCRIPTURAL CONTEXT

Whoever acknowledges me before others, I will also acknowledge before my Father in heaven. But whoever disowns me before others, I will disown before my Father in heaven (Matthew 10:32–33).

Fight the good fight of the faith. Take hold of the eternal life to which you were called when you made your good confession in the presence of many witnesses. . . . Keep this command without spot or blame until the appearing of our Lord Jesus Christ, which God will bring about in his own time—God, the blessed and only Ruler, the King of kings and Lord of lords. (1 Timothy 6:12, 14–15)

If anyone acknowledges that Jesus is the Son of God, God lives in them and they in God. (1 John 4:15)

For Further Study
Jeremiah 23:6
John 3:16
John 3:18
Acts 2:36
Romans 10:8–11
Romans 14:9
Ephesians 1:6
Ephesians 1:12

JOURNAL

Answer the following questions, and if you can place a specific date, even better: Have I repented truly of everything that separates me from God? Have I confessed all the sins I deliberately and knowingly committed? Is obeying God my priority?

_____

_____

_____

_____

_____

_____

_____

_____

_____

_____

_____

_____

_____

_____

_____

_____

_____

_____

PRAYER

Father, we want to proclaim that Jesus is Lord everywhere, not only with our words but also with who we are and what we do. We ask you to help us remain in holiness. Thank you for your great salvation.

46

TAKING CARE OF THE BEST GIFT

SCRIPTURE

Philippians 2:12

DEVOTIONAL REFLECTION

In Philippians 2:12 Paul repeats the "therefore" he uses in 2:1. It points to the previous expressions that present an antecedent that invites us to action.

In 2:5 Paul asks the Philippians to have the same mindset as Christ Jesus in their relationships with one another. And immediately he presents them with the seven steps of Jesus's exaltation. It starts with not considering equality with God and goes until complete humility to the point of death on a cross.

Paul explains that we should take care of Christ's saving work, which we have acquired by faith, working out our salvation with fear and trembling. We are saved only by faith because of the wonderful love of God asking his Son to pay for our sins, to transform us from inside out, to give us a pure heart, and to prepare us to serve him out of love. Once we have received the gift of salvation, we must take care of it with fear and trembling. It is a valuable gift we should take care of!

We are made for good works, not saved by works. God gave us life in abundance. We must take care of this life through prayer, reading the Word of God, worshiping with other believers, and sharing the love of God with others through acts of compassion. This is something natural for the believer. We cannot give ourselves the right of slipping away; we should be aware and assured in him. If we focus on worshiping God, we will hardly have time to slip away.

Scriptural Context

The wages of the righteous is life, but the earnings of the wicked are sin and death. (Proverbs 10:16)

Someone asked him, "Lord, are only a few people going to be saved?" He said to them, "Make every effort to enter through the narrow door, because many, I tell you, will try to enter and will not be able to." (Luke 13:23–24)

Do not work for food that spoils, but for food that endures to eternal life, which the Son of Man will give you. On him God the Father has placed his seal of approval. (John 6:27)

For we are God's workmanship, created in Christ Jesus to do good works, which God prepared in advance for us to do. (Ephesians 2:10)

We must pay the most careful attention, therefore, to what we have heard, so that we do not drift away. (Hebrews 2:1)

For Further Study
Matthew 11:12
1 Corinthians 9:24–27
Hebrews 4:9–11

Journal

How do you work out your salvation? Write about some ways we could disregard our salvation and lose it.

_____

_____

_____

_____

_____

_____

_____

_____

_____

_____

_____

_____

_____

_____

_____

_____

_____

_____

_____

_____

_____

_____

_____

_____

_____

_____

_____

_____

PRAYER

Holy Father, thank you for showing us your love and holiness in your
Son, Jesus. Thank you for the model of obedience that Jesus is for us.
Help us take care of the great treasure of salvation we have received with
fear and trembling, until the glorious coming of your Son, Jesus Christ.

47 ∿

THE ACTION OF MAINTAINING OURSELVES HOLY

SCRIPTURE
Philippians 2:12–13

DEVOTIONAL REFLECTION

Paul invites the Philippians and us to have the same attitude as Christ Jesus in Philippians 2:5. Then, from verses 6–11, he presents what many believe to be a hymn. After giving us the order and example, he then shows us how we can be like Christ.

The first thing Paul tells us is to do our part, taking care of our salvation with fear and trembling. This is the step that each human being should take. This is our part. We are not saved out of our own efforts, but we should take care of what we have received in grace.

Now Paul presents the second part. This one is incredible; it is God's part: "for it is God who works in you to will and to act in order to fulfill his good purpose." Many people are discouraged when they want to be saved out of their own efforts. It is as if they are in a hole and want to come out by grabbing their own hair. To be filled with the love of God, we need to receive the infilling of the Holy Spirit. God has given us spiritual victory. We should consider that both the help and the victory are spiritual.

God puts down walls when people obey! Being like Christ is the work of the Holy Spirit, not our own. Having victory and living like Christ is the work of the Holy Spirit in association with our will, in radical obedience to the Spirit who lives in us, obeying his voice and practicing the consciousness of his presence in our lives. This is the key for the abundant life: "for it is God who works in you to will and to act in order to fulfill his good purpose," and we simply associate ourselves with him and allow his power to act in us and through us, for his honor and glory.

Victory is possible when we allow the Holy Spirit to guide us and we do what he tells us to. An example would be to leave a place of privilege, or to leave a relationship. In a society, the participation of two parts is always needed. If God, through his Spirit, indicates that we must give up something in particular, we should make the decision to do it with his help. Many times, there is no victory because we have not surrendered our will.

SCRIPTURAL CONTEXT

Also in Judah the hand of God was on the people to give them unity of mind to carry out what the king and his officials had ordered, following the word of the LORD. (2 Chronicles 30:12)

LORD, you establish peace for us; all that we have accomplished you have done for us. (Isaiah 26:12)

To this John replied, "A person can receive only what is given them from heaven." (John 3:27)

No, in all these things we are more than conquerors through him who loved us. (Romans 8:37)

Every good and perfect gift is from above, coming down from the Father of the heavenly lights, who does not change like shifting shadows. He chose to give us birth through the word of truth, that we might be a kind of firstfruits of all he created. (James 1:17–18)

For Further Study
John 13:34–35
2 Corinthians 10:3–6
Ephesians 2:4–5
1 Thessalonians 5:23–24
Hebrews 13:20–21

JOURNAL

Describe the society we have with God. Explain Paul's phrase "for it is God who works in you to will and to act in order to fulfill his good purpose."

PRAYER

Thank you, Lord, for producing in us the desire to act according to your will. Help us align our will to your will, to obey in everything, knowing that you always desire the best for us.

48 &

Be Careful with Grumbling

Scripture
Philippians 2:12–14

Devotional Reflection

Paul has invited the Philippians and us to have the same mind and attitude of Christ, has shown the example of Christ (vv. 5–11), and now asks us to take care of our salvation with fear and trembling.

First, we have all the help of God: He is the One who "works in you to will and to act in order to fulfill his good purpose." God, intimately living in us through the Holy Spirit, places in us the desire to do his will. It is our part to put into practice God's desires. Then, Paul's first advice is to "do everything without grumbling or arguing." "Do everything" is an ample expression. It includes all the activities we are involved in, implying only what has to do with the will of God; that is, it takes for granted that we are not doing anything outside the will of God.

There are many examples of grumbling in the Bible. Grumbling does not please God. He does not like it, for it is against his will. God gives us works to do that correspond to the daily activities of life. Some of these are tedious, and many times we complain, saying, "Why do I have to do this?" We have to in order to learn humility, patience, consistency, professionalism, integrity, and wholeness. As we fulfill trivial activities that are common tasks within the will of God, he gives us more and more responsibility.

Grumbling and arguing are like a cancer that contaminates others; we become blinded to what God wants to do in our lives, and we ruin the reputation of Jesus among nonbelievers since they do not see Jesus represented by his ambassadors. One of the synonyms of grumbling is discredit. Maybe you have not realized it, but when you discredit someone without knowing him, you are also committing a fault.

SCRIPTURAL CONTEXT

In those days when the number of disciples was increasing, the Hellenistic Jews among them complained against the Hebraic Jews because their widows were being overlooked in the daily distribution of food. (Acts 6:1)

And do not grumble, as some of them did—and were killed by the destroying angel. These things happened to them as examples and were written down as warnings for us, on whom the fulfillment of the ages has come. (1 Corinthians 10:10–11)

May the Lord make your love increase and overflow for each other and for everyone else, just as ours does for you. (1 Thessalonians 3:12)

Don't grumble against each other, brothers, or you will be judged. The Judge is standing at the door! (James 5:9)

These men are grumblers and faultfinders; they follow their own evil desires; they boast about themselves and flatter others for their own advantage. (Jude 1:16)

For Further Study
Exodus 16:6–8
Numbers 14:27–29

JOURNAL

Explain the consequences of grumbling. Make a list of activities and labors you are doing that you do not like. Ask God for patience for these things and for God to help you not to grumble.

_____

_____

_____

_____

_____

_____

_____

_____

_____

_____

_____

_____

_____

_____

_____

_____

_____

_____

_____

_____

PRAYER

Father, help us put our eyes on Jesus. We ask your forgiveness if we
have deliberately spoken against somebody, and we beg you to help us
filter everything through your Holy Spirit. Father, help us leave all the
things we do not understand in your blessed hands for you to solve
them according to your will. Amen.

49

ALLOW JESUS TO SHINE THROUGH YOU

SCRIPTURE

Philippians 2:15

DEVOTIONAL REFLECTION

The expression "so that" with which verse 15 begins introduces the consequence of the actions in the previous verse. We do everything without grumbling *so that* we may become blameless and pure children of God. The absence of grumbling helps us not to have blemishes and to be pure. That is why our life is characterized by simplicity. The world's ostentation does not form part of the life of the believer.

We find ourselves in the midst of a "warped and crooked generation." Paul made this statement almost two thousand years ago. The contemporary morality is even more degenerated and more exposed through the means of communication. They reflect the consequences of abandoning biblical principles.

However, as believers and as a church, today we are like stars in the sky. It is in the midst of darkness that we shine. Let us not get it wrong; we are not the stars. We are the imperfect jars in which the treasure is placed, the bright Morning Star. As jars, we must be more and more transparent as time goes by. The thickness of the jar should become thinner (blameless and simple) over time so that the treasure, the bright Morning Star, shines more and more in the midst of a warped and crooked generation. A star shines all the time, not only when it is seen!

A light in the darkness serves as a guide. We, the children of God, have to guide others to give their hearts to Christ and not be lost.

SCRIPTURAL CONTEXT

Arise, shine, for your light has come, and the glory of the LORD *rises upon you. See, darkness covers the earth and thick darkness is over the peoples, but the* LORD *rises upon you and his glory appears over you. Nations will come to your light, and kings to the brightness of your dawn.* (Isaiah 60:1–3)

Where is the one who has been born king of the Jews? We saw his star in the east and have come to worship him. (Matthew 2:2)

For God, who said, "Let light shine out of darkness," made his light shine in our hearts to give us the light of the knowledge of the glory of God in the face of Christ. But we have this treasure in jars of clay to show that this all-surpassing power is from God and not from us. (2 Corinthians 4:6–7)

For Further Study
Numbers 24:17
Matthew 2:10–11
Ephesians 5:8–14
Revelation 2:26–29
Revelation 22:16–17

JOURNAL

In what way can we shine in the midst of moral darkness? Think of some ways in which Jesus can shine through you in your home, in your workplace, in your school, and among your friends and acquaintances. Write them down in the following lines.

_____

_____

_____

_____

_____

_____

_____

Prayer

Holy Father, continue to work in our lives, in our jars of clay, so that every day, every hour, every moment, we can allow your Son to shine more and more through us.

50

SHINING IN THE DARKNESS

SCRIPTURE

Philippians 2:14–16

DEVOTIONAL REFLECTION

The central aspect of the whole letter to the Philippians is the incredible example of Jesus Christ, who gave up everything even to the point of dying on the cross for us. Paul invites his readers to be like Jesus, to have the same way of thinking, to have the same attitude, and to collaborate with Jesus in the best of causes—rescuing many who are in the darkness. That is why, when we face difficult situations, we should ask ourselves the question, *What would Jesus do in my place?*

Paul immediately offers practical advice about how to have the mind of Jesus. The first is to live free of grumbling and arguing. The second is to "hold firmly to the word of life." The word "hold" is interesting. In the original Greek, it is made up of two words. The first means "over," and the second means "grab." The second piece of advice Paul gives us literally means to place ourselves "over" the Word and "grab" it with all our strength. It is not an amulet; it is a book. What is written in it is the guide to all truth and counsel of God.

When and where should we hold on to the Word of God? Philippians 2:15 gives us the context of this action—in the midst of a warped and crooked generation.

There are millions of books, and many of them are excellent. However, none can replace the Bible. We are in the world, but we are not of the world. We are in the midst of alarming situations, surrounded by immorality and consumerism. We are in a world full of lies, threats, wars, and evil people who want to harm us. That is where God has sent us to shine like stars, to rescue those who are lost.

We begin by avoiding grumbling and arguing in our own lives. A person who is not involved in grumbling and arguing is healthy and trustworthy. The only way to be like Jesus in the midst of darkness is to shine like him, by holding on to his Word. That means holding on to Jesus himself, having his life in my life, his Word, the Bible. The result is life, and life in abundance (see John 10:10), or stars in the sky in the midst of a warped and crooked generation.

SCRIPTURAL CONTEXT

Since my youth, O God, you have taught me, and to this day I declare your marvelous deeds. Even when I am old and gray, do not forsake me, O God, till I declare your power to the next generation, your might to all who are to come. Your righteousness reaches to the skies, O God, you who have done great things. Who, O God, is like you? (Psalm 71:17–19)

The Spirit gives life; the flesh counts for nothing. The words I have spoken to you are spirit and they are life. (John 6:63)

If it is possible, as far as it depends on you, live at peace with everyone. (Romans 12:18)

Make every effort to live in peace with all men and to be holy; without holiness no one will see the Lord. (Hebrews 12:14)

For Further Study
John 17:14–17
Romans 10:8–11
2 Timothy 2:15–16
Hebrews 4:10–13

JOURNAL

Make a plan about how you will read and study the Bible. Establish clear goals, the place where you will read, and the way in which you will study the Word.

_____

_____

_____

_____

_____

_____

_____

_____

_____

_____

_____

_____

_____

_____

_____

_____

_____

_____

_____

_____

_____

_____

_____

PRAYER

Lord, I hold on to you, to your holy Word. Help me read it and understand it, and to apply it to my life, relationships, behavior, and mind. Lord, shine through me!

51

DISCIPLE SOMEONE

SCRIPTURE
Philippians 2:16–18

DEVOTIONAL REFLECTION
Paul received a clear mission from the Lord Jesus Christ (see Acts 26:16–18). Today, Jesus also tells you: *Get up! Continue with the mission God gave you when he called you to minister.* The problems or discouragements of life cannot turn off the voice of Jesus saying, "Get up!"

After many missionary journeys, Paul ended up in prison in Rome. There, he discipled the guards. But what about the disciples he left in Philippi and in other cities? That is the reason he wrote letters to them. Now he tells them to put into practice what they have received in writing. His goal is not to run or labor in vain.

Paul has made the decision to invest all his strength to fulfill the purpose of God for his life. Paul does not do this on his own strength, but "struggling with all God's energy."

Paul uses all possible means to disciple. He disciples those who are close to him, establishes them in a local church, and finds other disciplers for them. He also writes letters to them and stays in contact with them. His letters are passed around among disciple leaders and believers. Without a doubt, it is the greatest leadership strategy of that time!

Paul has a conviction that winning the nonbelievers is not enough; he wants a discipleship system so the believers will grow in the doctrine in order to be trained and established in ministry. By being involved in their lives, he tells the Philippians: "I am glad and rejoice with all of you. So you too should be glad and rejoice with me."

Scriptural Context

To be a minister of Christ Jesus to the Gentiles with the priestly duty of proclaiming the gospel of God, so that the Gentiles might become an offering acceptable to God, sanctified by the Holy Spirit. (Romans 15:16)

So I will very gladly spend for you everything I have and expend myself as well. If I love you more, will you love me less? (2 Corinthians 12:15)

For this reason, when I could stand it no longer, I sent to find out about your faith. I was afraid that in some way the tempter might have tempted you and our efforts might have been useless. (1 Thessalonians 3:5)

And the things you have heard me say in the presence of many witnesses entrust to reliable men who will also be qualified to teach others. (2 Timothy 2:2)

For I am already being poured out like a drink offering, and the time has come for my departure. I have fought the good fight, I have finished the race, I have kept the faith. (2 Timothy 4:6–7)

For Further Study
1 Corinthians 9:26–27
Colossians 1:27–29

Journal

Make a list of people in whom you could invest your life in the following weeks.

_____

_____

_____

_____

_____

_____

_____

_____

_____

_____

_____

_____

_____

_____

_____

_____

_____

_____

_____

_____

_____

_____

_____

_____

_____

_____

_____

_____

_____

_____

PRAYER

Lord, help us to clearly understand the purpose you have for our lives and to dedicate all our strength to fulfill that purpose. Help us to do it in the power of your Spirit and not on our own strength.

52

HOPE AND PERSONAL AFFAIRS

SCRIPTURE
Philippians 2:23–24

DEVOTIONAL REFLECTION
Paul is a man of hope. In Colossians, Paul presents three types of hope: Future hope (Colossians 1:5); present hope (Colossians 1:23); and hope that is trustworthy (Colossians 1:27). Even though Paul is sure of his hope in Jesus, knowing he has an eternal guarantee, Paul also takes care of his personal life, his way of living, and his circumstances. Paul is convinced that he will get out of prison. Even in horrible circumstances, he does not lose hope.

As believers, we must have hope and share hope. We should know who our hope is. No matter what our circumstances are, we should know that God is in control and that everything that happens is for our well-being, even though it might not seem so in that moment.

Together with Paul, we can say that our future is assured.

SCRIPTURAL CONTEXT
That is why I am suffering as I am. Yet this is no cause for shame, because I know whom I have believed, and am convinced that he is able to guard what I have entrusted to him for that day. (2 Timothy 1:12)

At my first defense, no one came to my support, but everyone deserted me. May it not be held against them. But the Lord stood at my side and gave me strength, so that through me the message might be fully proclaimed and all the Gentiles might hear it. And I was delivered from the lion's mouth. (2 Timothy 4:16–17)

So after I have completed this task and have made sure that they have received this fruit, I will go to Spain and visit you on the way. I know that when I come to you, I will come in the full measure of the blessing of Christ. (Romans 15:28–29)

For Further Study
Philippians 1:25–26
Colossians 1:5
Colossians 1:23
Colossians 1:27

JOURNAL
Define the three types of hope that Paul has, using the Colossians texts referenced. As you read the rest of the verses in the Scriptural Context section, make a declaration of what it means in practice to have God's hope in your life.

_____

_____

_____

_____

_____

_____

_____

_____

_____

_____

_____

_____

_____

PRAYER
Lord, we surrender the control to you of any situation that might be happening. We rely on you, the Rock of eternity, our safe refuge, and who helps us in times of need. Thank you for giving us present and future hope, and the knowledge that we are safe in Jesus.

53
FAITHFUL DISCIPLE

SCRIPTURE
Philippians 2:25–30

DEVOTIONAL REFLECTION
Paul has mentioned his disciple Timothy and explained to the Philippians the type of person he is—a good disciple and a servant leader. Now he introduces another disciple, Epaphroditus. This man is a member of the congregation in Philippi. He went to visit Paul in Rome, and during his visit "he was ill, and almost died. But God had mercy on him." Paul sends Epaphroditus back to Philippi with the letter we are reading now.

Epaphroditus shows us some of the characteristics of a faithful disciple: 1) He is a Christian. Above anything, a disciple has to be converted and be a faithful follower of Christ. 2) A faithful disciple is a servant. He is willing to do whatever is required of him and is always ready to respond to needs and minister in the church in various areas. 3) A disciple is a disciplined, systematic person who risks his life for the mission of spreading the good news. But above all, he is a companion God has placed beside another faithful soldier. 4) He is someone who is sent to take the good news. He is the person who comes to Philippi to bring the offering of the Philippians to Paul. He is a carrier of good news and mercy. 5) He is a merciful person who shepherds even his leaders. He went to minister to the apostle Paul. Paul says of him, "He risked his life to make up for the help you yourselves could not give me." Finally Paul says that this disciple, Epaphroditus, is 6) a living example of Christ.

With the passing of time and in this era of so much consumerism, sometimes the church is confused with an enterprise, or even worse, it is considered a department of the government, where protocols must be followed in order to satisfy the egos of a few. Paul does not send his employee; he sends his fellow, his mate who is willing to give everything for love, the same love that Paul shows in his words when he talks about him.

Scriptural Context

Like the coolness of snow at harvest time is a trustworthy messenger to those who send him; he refreshes the spirit of his masters. (Proverbs 25:13)

How beautiful on the mountains are the feet of those who bring good news, who proclaim peace, who bring good tidings, who proclaim salvation, who say to Zion, "Your God reigns!" (Isaiah 52:7)

As you sent me into the world, I have sent them into the world. (John 17:18)

How, then, can they call on the one they have not believed in? And how can they believe in the one of whom they have not heard? And how can they hear without someone preaching to them? And how can anyone preach unless they are sent? As it is written: "How beautiful are the feet of those who bring good news!" (Romans 10:14–15)

Epaphras, my fellow prisoner in Christ Jesus, sends you greetings. And so do Mark, Aristarchus, Demas and Luke, my fellow workers. (Philemon 1:23–24)

For Further Study
Romans 15:12
Philippians 4:18
2 Timothy 2:3–4

Journal

If someone is talking about you and describing you as a disciple, could that person refer to you with the same characteristics as that of Epaphroditus? How do you speak of other disciples of Christ? Are you aware that the love of God should be reflected in the opinions you offer about others? Write your thoughts.

_____

_____

_____

_____

_____

_____

_____

_____

_____

_____

_____

_____

_____

_____

_____

_____

_____

_____

_____

_____

_____

_____

PRAYER

Lord, help us to be faithful disciples like Timothy and Epaphroditus,
that, along with others, we may serve you with faithfulness and joy.

UNIT 3
DANGERS IN THE CHURCH

54

CONTINUED TEACHING

SCRIPTURE
Philippians 3:1–3

DEVOTIONAL REFLECTION
Chapter 3 of Philippians starts with a positive declaration. Chapter 2 took us to heavenly places by showing us Christ's mindset and the vitality of two disciples, Timothy and Epaphroditus. Now Paul moves on to touch on a problem in the church. He begins by stating an important principle, that of teaching the foundations of faith once again. It is about not only making sure the believers have the mindset of Christ but also that they are being discipled and receiving constant instruction.

Paul wants the members of the church in Philippi not to be misled by workers who impose other doctrines that are not part of the gospel, such as circumcision and fleshly alterations of the faith. When the people of God stop receiving training from the Word of God, it is possible to fall into the hands of people who want to cause division. That is why the Bible should be our main book and its teachings should be our principles of life.

Paul's word of exhortation is very strong. He calls everyone who deviates the believers from the good doctrine dogs, evildoers, and mutilators of the flesh. Through the centuries, the church has always been exposed to these types of people. The duty of the church is to stay away, to watch out and not be contaminated.

A constant characteristic that is found in these dogs, evildoers, and mutilators of the flesh is that they try to satisfy the carnal nature, the desires of the flesh, by imposing traditions and seeking the satisfaction of their emotions. The antidote Paul recommends is to live as those "who serve God by his Spirit, who boast in Christ Jesus." That is, the service to God is in the power of the Spirit, and the results are for the glory of God and Christ. That is also the indicator of the legitimacy of the workers.

SCRIPTURAL CONTEXT

He must hold firmly to the trustworthy message as it has been taught, so that he can encourage others by sound doctrine and refute those who oppose it. (Titus 1:9)

In fact, though by this time you ought to be teachers, you need someone to teach you the elementary truths of God's word all over again. You need milk, not solid food! (Hebrews 5:12)

But solid food is for the mature, who by constant use have trained themselves to distinguish good from evil. (Hebrews 5:14)

So I will always remind you of these things, even though you know them and are firmly established in the truth you now have. (2 Peter 1:12)

Dear friends, this is now my second letter to you. I have written both of them as reminders to stimulate you to wholesome thinking. I want you to recall the words spoken in the past by the holy prophets and the command given by our Lord and Savior through your apostles. (2 Peter 3:1–2)

JOURNAL

List the advice Paul gives in order to have a healthy church.

_____

_____

_____

_____

_____

_____

_____

_____

_____

_____

_____

_____

_____

_____

_____

_____

_____

_____

_____

_____

_____

_____

_____

_____

_____

_____

_____

_____

_____

PRAYER

Holy Father, keep your church alert to the dogs and the evil workers. Protect us and help us see signs of those who want to be glorified. Help us battle them in prayer, in the Spirit, for our weapons are not fleshly ones.

55 ❧
TRUST IN WHAT CANNOT BE TRUSTED

SCRIPTURE
Philippians 3:4–7

DEVOTIONAL REFLECTION

Paul presents a new concept to the Philippians. He presents what it means to "trust in the flesh": trust in oneself, trust in what you have achieved, trust in your lineage, trust in your social position, trust in your leadership status, trust in your character, or trust in your personality. We all have something to trust in. Throughout the years, we build our lives, our treasures, our strategies to move ahead, and our way to show who we are. Paul's concept of living in the flesh means more than just living in a physical body; it means depending on what we have constructed on our own, what we have created to survive in the midst of a world that encloses us, pressures us, and wants to take us and shake us. We have grown up surviving in the flesh.

In 1 Corinthians 2 and 3, Paul speaks of three types of people: a) the natural person (1 Corinthians 2:14); b) the carnal person (1 Corinthians 3:1); and c) the spiritual person (1 Corinthians 2:15).

In Romans 8, Paul presents two modes of existing: according to the flesh and according to the Spirit. He tells us we can live depending on our achievements, or we can live depending on the Holy Spirit. It depends on us to decide every second and moment by moment.

In Galatians 5, Paul presents the consequences (or the fruit) of living either according to the flesh or according to the Spirit. It can be a life full of bitterness, inconsistency, and fruitlessness or a life full of love, joy, peace, and fullness.

Paul has reasons to glory in the flesh, but he makes a radical decision.

Scriptural Context

Those who live according to the flesh have their minds set on what the flesh desires; but those who live in accordance with the Spirit have their minds set on what the Spirit desires. The mind governed by the flesh is death, but the mind governed by the Spirit is life and peace. (Romans 8:5–6)

Brothers and sisters, I could not address you as people who live by the Spirit but as people who are still worldly—mere infants in Christ. I gave you milk, not solid food, for you were not yet ready for it. Indeed, you are still not ready. (1 Corinthians 3:1–2)

Those who belong to Christ Jesus have crucified the flesh with its passions and desires. Since we live by the Spirit, let us keep in step with the Spirit. (Galatians 5:24–25)

For Further Study
2 Corinthians 11:18–21
Galatians 5:16–23

Journal

Describe in the following lines what it means to live according to the flesh as opposed to living according to the Spirit. Give an example of each way of life.

_____

_____

_____

_____

_____

_____

_____

_____

_____

_____

_____

_____

_____

_____

_____

_____

_____

_____

_____

_____

_____

_____

_____

_____

_____

_____

_____

_____

_____

_____

_____

_____

PRAYER

Lord, help us to be spiritual in everything, not to live by the flesh or for the flesh. Help us to live according to your strength and your Spirit, and in that way bear fruit in the Spirit.

56
DEPENDENCE

SCRIPTURE
Philippians 3:4, 7

DEVOTIONAL REFLECTION

The first thing Paul does to ensure success in his ministry is to regard whatever were formerly gains to him as "loss for the sake of Christ." He means achievements he gained through his own strength or because of his circumstances in life—things that could help him trust in the flesh. When we esteem something, we give it value. Everything Paul gained in the flesh, he now considers loss. This ideology reflects the exact opposite of the world, which only seeks to highlight and exhibit the achievements we've attained.

Many aspects of the past will not help in the future. We must give thanks to God for our achievements and for the circumstances of our life, whatever they are, because it is God who allowed those things to happen.

When Paul says he now considers them loss, it doesn't mean a total abandonment of achievements and titles. It means he does not depend on such achievements or things. Paul has decided that God will take all of his past life, all of his achievements and studies, and use them for the kingdom if he wants to. Paul does not rely on his scholarship, his skills in language, or his lineage to extend the kingdom.

It is important for all of our gifts and talents to be consecrated to God, and for us to recognize that we have them because of his grace, to be used for his service. Paul allows God to use all of that, but he depends on the power of God. His life motivation is for the sake of Christ.

SCRIPTURAL CONTEXT

Then the LORD said to Satan, "Have you considered my servant Job? There is no one on earth like him; he is blameless and upright, a man who fears God and shuns evil. And he still maintains his integrity, though you incited me against him to ruin him without any reason." "Skin for skin!" Satan replied. "A man will give all he has for his own life. But now stretch out your hand and strike his flesh and bones, and he will surely curse you to your face." (Job 2:3–5)

A person's riches may ransom their life, but the poor cannot respond to threatening rebukes. (Proverbs 13:8)

And whoever does not carry their cross and follow me cannot be my disciple. (Luke 14:27)

To this end I strenuously contend with all the energy Christ so powerfully works in me. (Colossians 1:29)

JOURNAL

It is interesting to make a list of all our achievements and life situations in order to evaluate them. How can this help me or hinder me in fulfilling the purpose of God for my life? Give some examples from your personal life.

_____

_____

_____

_____

_____

_____

_____

_____

_____

PRAYER

Lord, thank you for all the achievements of the past and also for the ones we will receive from your hand in the future. Thank you for allowing us to receive so much without deserving it. Help us depend only on you, and use our experiences and our circumstances for your purposes, not for our own.

57

PURPOSE

SCRIPTURE

Philippians 3:7–8

DEVOTIONAL REFLECTION

The first step of Paul's ministerial career is dependence. He does not depend on himself, his past, his achievements, or his family. He does not depend on anything earthly. He not only considers everything loss. Now he makes an even stronger declaration. Everything vanishes, and whatever little he has gained, he regards as garbage.

Paul is not a renegade or a masochist who wants to suffer. Paul has the highest goal any person could have—gaining Christ. Paul's purpose is to know Christ. He is not talking about mental knowledge, and he is not talking about buying Christ. Here he is expressing the maximum desire of intimacy with Jesus, of being close to him, of not losing him, of treasuring him, of gaining him.

These names are the ones that Paul uses to present Jesus, and they show who Jesus is to Paul: a) Christ Jesus: the Galilean, the Man, the Deliverer (Messiah), Liberator; b) Lord: Paul's Master, his Owner, his God, his Love.

Jesus Christ the Lord is the only purpose and reason for everything Paul does.

SCRIPTURAL CONTEXT

I consider that our present sufferings are not worth comparing with the glory that will be revealed in us. (Romans 8:18)

So it is with you. Since you are eager for gifts of the Spirit, try to excel in those that build up the church. (1 Corinthians 14:12)

And to know this love that surpasses knowledge—that you may be filled to the measure of all the fullness of God. (Ephesians 3:19)

For I am already being poured out like a drink offering, and the time for my departure is near. I have fought the good fight, I have finished the race, I have kept the faith. Now there is in store for me the crown of righteousness, which the Lord, the righteous Judge, will award to me on that day—and not only to me, but also to all who have longed for his appearing. (2 Timothy 4:6–8)

For Further Study
Psalm 126:5–6
Luke 10:21–22
1 Corinthians 2:2–4
1 John 5:20

JOURNAL

The second step of Paul's success is having a spiritual purpose based on the will of God. Write down what Paul's purpose in life is. Then, in prayer, write down what your purpose in life is.

_____

_____

_____

_____

_____

_____

_____

_____

_____

_____

_____

_____

_____

_____

_____

_____

_____

_____

_____

_____

_____

_____

_____

_____

_____

_____

_____

_____

_____

_____

_____

_____

_____

PRAYER

Lord, thank you for the testimony of the apostle Paul. Thank you because you are always his priority in everything. Help us, Lord, to have
you as our purpose in everything.

58 ❧
FOUND IN CHRIST

SCRIPTURE
Philippians 3:9

DEVOTIONAL REFLECTION

"In him" is one of the most important phrases in Paul's writings. It is the synonym of being baptized with the Holy Spirit. "In him" is the condition of being submerged and saturated in the Holy Spirit in such a way that any word, action, thought, or attitude spills over to others in Jesus. Being saturated in him, we reflect the justice or righteousness of God. We reflect the same mindset as Christ Jesus. Life in him, Paul says, is only possible by faith. Faith is to believe in what cannot be seen (see Hebrews 11:1).

Our justice or righteousness is the result of God's life in us. It is by faith, and it consists in living 24 hours a day, 365 days a year, submerged in him. It is all about him, and it is all on the basis of faith. As we are submerged in him, we live by faith. Therefore, in that moment, we will be found in him, not only on the day of his second coming and at the final judgment, but also today in every word, in every attitude, in every circumstance, all the time!

When we are submerged in the Spirit of God, there is no more space for any work of the flesh.

SCRIPTURAL CONTEXT

My mouth will tell of your righteous deeds, of your saving acts all day long— though I know not how to relate them all. I will come and proclaim your mighty acts, Sovereign LORD; I will proclaim your righteous deeds, yours alone. Since my youth, God, you have taught me, and to this day I declare your marvelous deeds. (Psalm 71:15–17)

For in the gospel the righteousness of God is revealed—a righteousness that is by faith from first to last, just as it is written: "The righteous will live by faith." (Romans 1:17)

It is because of him that you are in Christ Jesus, who has become for us wisdom from God—that is, our righteousness, holiness and redemption. Therefore, as it is written: "Let the one who boasts boast in the Lord." (1 Corinthians 1:30–31)

For Further Study
John 10:10
John 16:8–11
Galatians 2:16

JOURNAL

What does Paul mean by the expression "in him"? How would you apply it to the daily aspects of your life?

_____

_____

_____

_____

_____

_____

_____

_____

_____

_____

PRAYER

Lord, help me every day so that in every circumstance, attitude, and action in my life I may be found in you.

59 MARTYRDOM?

SCRIPTURE
Philippians 3:9–10

DEVOTIONAL REFLECTION

If we are in Christ, we do not live for ourselves. Not living for ourselves means living in a new sphere of life.

Jesus was the only one worthy of dying for the sins of humanity. I will never be like him in his death by dying on a cross. Only Jesus is the Savior. Being like him is the defeat of my sovereignty over my own life and ministry. It means to take the attitude of a servant. It means to have the mindset of Christ. Becoming like him in his death means to be like Christ in his eternal relationship with God and in his relationships as he lived as the second Adam, being radical and extreme until death, in order to know the Father and obey his will.

Becoming like him in his death means to adopt the life, the word, and the obedience of Jesus Christ for our life. Becoming like him in his death begins with a complete consecration that shows us clearly what the will of God is. Becoming like him in his death is not imitating Christ; it is allowing him, who resides in my life, to become the president of everything in my life; for him to love through me; for him to forgive through me; for him to live through me. Becoming like him in his death is allowing God, through Jesus, by the power of the Holy Spirit, to produce fruit in me.

SCRIPTURAL CONTEXT

Then he said to them all: "Whoever wants to be my disciple must deny themselves and take up their cross daily and follow me. For whoever wants to save their life will lose it, but whoever loses their life for me will save it." (Luke 9:23–24)

I face death every day—yes, just as surely as I boast about you in Christ Jesus our Lord. (1 Corinthians 15:31)

For just as we share abundantly in the sufferings of Christ, so also our comfort abounds through Christ. (2 Corinthians 1:5)

Therefore, if anyone is in Christ, the new creation has come: The old has gone, the new is here! (2 Corinthians 5:17)

I have been crucified with Christ and I no longer live, but Christ lives in me. The life I now live in the body, I live by faith in the Son of God, who loved me and gave himself for me (Galatians 2:20).

For Further Study
Matthew 20:23
John 12:24–25
Romans 6:3–5
Romans 8:29
Romans 12:1–2
2 Corinthians 4:10–11
2 Corinthians 5:15

JOURNAL

Give some practical examples from your daily life to show how you can become like Christ in his death.

_____

_____

_____

_____

_____

_____

_____

_____

_____

_____

_____

_____

_____

_____

_____

_____

_____

_____

_____

_____

_____

_____

_____

_____

_____

_____

_____

_____

PRAYER

"Not my will, but thine; not my will, but thine; not my will, but thy will be done, Lord in me. May thy Spirit divine fill this being of mine. Not my will, but thy will be done, Lord, in me." (*Sing to the Lord*, Church of the Nazarene Hymnal, #491)

60

TWO DEATHS, ONE RESURRECTION

SCRIPTURE
Philippians 3:9, 11

DEVOTIONAL REFLECTION

To be found in Jesus is one of the most important concepts in Scripture for the victorious and full life of the Christian. Paul does not doubt his salvation for one second, nor the victory he has in Christ. Paul knows that, apart from Jesus, he can do nothing.

When Paul says, "and so, somehow, attaining to the resurrection from the dead," he in no way doubts his salvation. This expression shows Paul's confidence that only in being found in Jesus can we remain in certainty, firmness, and with the hope of glory.

When we confess our sins and decide to abandon sin with all of our strength, we repent and live righteously and in holiness. When we know him more and more every day, we experience the power of his resurrection. Then we have the certainty that our names are written in the Book of Life, for we are cleansed of all sin, saved from eternal death, and live with the hope of life, living the abundant life!

However, whoever abandons Jesus and returns to sin and is not found in Christ does not abide in him when the day of the second coming comes, or on the day of their death. They will go to hell and participate in the second death and will be condemned eternally.

Along with Paul, we have the hope that, because of the love and power of Jesus in us, coupled with obedience and faithfulness to God, we will somehow attain to the resurrection from the dead. Jesus does not leave things undone; allow him to continue to work in you.

Scriptural Context

Jesus said to her, "I am the resurrection and the life. The one who believes in me will live, even though they die; and whoever lives by believing in me will never die. Do you believe this?" (John 11:25–26)

If you keep my commands, you will remain in my love, just as I have kept my Father's commands and remain in his love. (John 15:10)

Therefore, since we have been justified through faith, we have peace with God through our Lord Jesus Christ, through whom we have gained access by faith into this grace in which we now stand. And we boast in the hope of the glory of God. (Romans 5:2)

Whoever has ears, let them hear what the Spirit says to the churches. The one who is victorious will not be hurt at all by the second death. (Revelation 2:11)

Blessed and holy are those who share in the first resurrection. The second death has no power over them, but they will be priests of God and of Christ and will reign with him for a thousand years. (Revelation 20:6)

For Further Study
Matthew 10:22
Luke 20:35
Romans 8:38–39
1 Corinthians 9:26–27
2 Timothy 4:6–8
Hebrews 11:35
Revelation 20:14–15

JOURNAL

Explain the title of this devotional. What does "two deaths, one resurrection" mean?

_____

_____

_____

_____

_____

_____

_____

_____

_____

_____

_____

_____

_____

_____

_____

_____

_____

PRAYER

Holy Father, thank you for giving us Jesus, the hope of glory, who sustains us and keeps us victorious as we are transformed from glory to glory. Help us to hold on to him so that we may be safe, firm, and abiding in Jesus until our death or his second coming.

61

THE PRIZE OF THE SUPREME CALLING OF GOD IN CHRIST JESUS

SCRIPTURE
Philippians 3:12–14

DEVOTIONAL REFLECTION

Paul begins verse 12 by talking about his own humanity. Being fallible and finite, he does not allow his humanity to become something negative. On the contrary, he focuses on the goal to win the prize for which God has called him heavenward in Christ Jesus.

Luke explains in the book of Acts how Paul, on his way to Rome to his final prison, still has a very clear understanding of what his heavenward calling is. Paul takes actions that help us today as guidelines to fulfill the purpose of God for our lives. Paul knows who he is, and he understands his human situation. He knows what God has done in him and the provision of God for him. Paul focuses on the call of God and makes it his priority.

He also decides to reject Satan's accusations about his past. He rejects living in the achievements and triumphs of the past. He also rejects his history and personal accomplishments. There is nothing sadder for a child of God than to be stuck in past achievements. The almighty God who lives and reigns is by your side for you to continue the race you have ahead of you. He has called you and backs you up. Do not stop! The children of God do not retire. It is our duty to preach the gospel of Christ until our very last breath, for if we live, it is for him, and if we die, we die for him.

Paul is proactive, and as a runner getting to the end of the race, he continues to press on toward the goal. The goal is nothing more and nothing less than Jesus himself.

SCRIPTURAL CONTEXT

The LORD will vindicate me; your love, LORD, endures forever—do not abandon the works of your hands. (Psalm 138:8)

But when completeness comes, what is in part disappears. (1 Corinthians 13:10)

Therefore, since we have these promises, dear friends, let us purify ourselves from everything that contaminates body and spirit, perfecting holiness out of reverence for God. (2 Corinthians 7:1)

Now may the God of peace, who through the blood of the eternal covenant brought back from the dead our Lord Jesus, that great Shepherd of the sheep, equip you with everything good for doing his will, and may he work in us what is pleasing to him, through Jesus Christ, to whom be glory for ever and ever. Amen. (Hebrews 13:20–21)

In fact, this is love for God: to keep his commands. And his commands are not burdensome. (1 John 5:3)

For Further Study
Psalm 42:1–2
Psalm 63:7–8
Acts 26:15–19
Romans 15:23–24
1 Corinthians 9:24–27
1 Peter 5:10–11

JOURNAL

Do you remember what God called you for? Are you willing to reach the goal? What is your focus in order to reach the goal?

_____

_____

_____

_____

_____

_____

_____

_____

_____

_____

_____

_____

_____

_____

_____

_____

_____

_____

_____

_____

_____

_____

_____

_____

_____

_____

_____

_____

PRAYER

Father, help us to run with patience. Help us to focus only on Jesus, and to have the discipline to fulfill the supreme calling, believing with all our hearts that you will never leave us alone.

62

NOT PERFECT YET

SCRIPTURE
Philippians 3:12, 15

DEVOTIONAL REFLECTION

In these verses, it seems as though Paul is contradicting himself. The old NIV uses the word "perfect" in verse 12. Paul is talking about two different kinds of perfection. The word "perfection" in the original language is *teleios*, and it means "having completed its end goal or purpose," or, something that is used for the purpose for which it was created. For example, a pencil was made for writing. If we use it to dig a hole in the earth, it is not fulfilling its purpose. But if it is a used pencil, one that is worn out, it has been used for the purpose it was created. It is "perfect;" it is *teleios*.

Perfection in the New and Old Testament is also defined as purity of heart. Søren Kierkegaard defines purity of heart as "to will one thing." Purity of heart or perfection is to only desire God, and nothing else. When we desire only God, we will be living to the praise of his glory, for we will only do his will, his purpose for our lives.

Purity is the absence of something that is alien to a substance or compound. We stop being pure when we are contaminated by sin. When God fills us with his Holy Spirit, or as Paul puts it, when we are found in Christ, he purifies us. He takes away double intentions, we no longer serve two masters, and we no longer have hearts that are otherwise minded.

Is Paul contradicting himself? No! There are two types of perfection. *Teleios* perfection, which Paul talks about, indicates that Paul is fulfilling the purpose of his life. His heart only desires to be found in Christ.

Paul is a person just like us. He has many weaknesses. He has a rough character; he is quite hasty and has several conflicts with some companions (see Acts 15:39; Galatians 2:11–14). On a certain occasion, Paul even fails on a missionary trip (see 2 Corinthians 2:12–13). So is Paul perfect? Yes and no! He is pure of heart, he is in Christ, and he wants to be found in him all the time. He is being used for the purpose for which God created him. But he is human, fragile, finite, and imperfect like all of us. It is for that reason that he chooses to be disciplined (see 1 Corinthians 9:27).

Many times we make mistakes, and sometimes they are serious ones, whether or not that was our intent. Many people say, "We are not perfect; we are human!" But as we are human beings who make mistakes, we should also be human beings who ask for forgiveness. God speaks to us, and we run to the throne of grace to find the relief we need. Perfection of heart—purity of heart—is not an option; it is a command (see Genesis 17:1 and Matthew 5:48). It is not about our achievement or discipline; it is about God's grace over us.

SCRIPTURAL CONTEXT

This is the account of Noah and his family. Noah was a righteous man, blameless among the people of his time, and he walked faithfully with God. (Genesis 6:9)

You must be blameless before the LORD your God. (Deuteronomy 18:13)

In the land of Uz there lived a man whose name was Job. This man was blameless and upright; he feared God and shunned evil. (Job 1:1)

Jesus answered, "If you want to be perfect, go, sell your possessions and give to the poor, and you will have treasure in heaven. Then come, follow me." (Matthew 19:21)

My dear children, I write this to you so that you will not sin. But if anybody does sin, we have an advocate with the Father—Jesus Christ, the Righteous One. He is the atoning sacrifice for our sins, and not only for ours but also for the sins of the whole world. (1 John 2:1–2)

For Further Study
Genesis 17:1
1 Kings 11:4
Matthew 5:48
Ephesians 4:13
Hebrews 7:28
James 3:2

JOURNAL

How would you define a double-minded person? What difference
does it make to say that purity of heart is an order and not an option?
What does the text refer to when it speaks about perfection or purity
of heart? In what sense are we pure of intent and at the same time not
perfect since we are finite and make mistakes?

PRAYER

Lord, thank you for living in us, for filling us with your fullness, for
purifying our hearts, and for giving us perfect intentions. We beg you
to continue to speak to us and correct us since we are fragile jars of clay.
Give us more and more sensitivity to hear your voice and obey in everything even though we still make mistakes. Help us change whatever
could hurt others or be a stumbling block in kingdom advancement.

63 🌿
TESTIMONY + UNITY = EFFECTIVE DISCIPLESHIP

SCRIPTURE
Philippians 3:12, 15

DEVOTIONAL REFLECTION
After Paul explains that he is fulfilling the purpose of God for his life, he speaks of what God has done in his life. God has given him purity of heart to make disciples who are also pure of heart. The next thing Paul does is to invite the Philippians to have the mind of Christ, to "take such a view of things." The key to effective discipleship is unity of purpose, plus a good testimony.

Once we know what the patterns of conduct of God are, and once we live them, we can ask our disciples to follow us. Meanwhile, we should not ask someone to do something we ourselves do not do or would not do. The next step is for them to look for people of testimony, those who are willing to have unity of purpose; then there will be effective discipleship.

SCRIPTURAL CONTEXT
Live in harmony with one another. Do not be proud, but be willing to associate with people of low position. Do not be conceited. Do not repay anyone evil for evil. Be careful to do what is right in the eyes of everyone. If it is possible, as far as it depends on you, live at peace with everyone. (Romans 12:16–18)

Follow my example, as I follow the example of Christ. (1 Corinthians 11:1)

And the things you have heard me say in the presence of many witnesses entrust to reliable people who will also be qualified to teach others. (2 Timothy 2:2)

For Further Study
Romans 15:5–6
Galatians 5:7
Hebrews 10:38–39

JOURNAL

Explain biblical discipleship according to the above text. What is the first step for you to disciple another person?

_____

_____

_____

_____

_____

_____

_____

_____

_____

_____

_____

_____

_____

_____

PRAYER

Lord, help me be obedient in everything, to represent you rather than myself. Help others to desire to be like you when they get to know me. Help me be an example in every situation and aspect of my life. Lord, help us be faithful to have faithful disciples who follow you, and help us to continue making disciples.

64 ᔧ
ENEMIES OF CHRIST

SCRIPTURE
Philippians 3:18–19

DEVOTIONAL REFLECTION

This is a sad passage. Paul writes "with tears." He speaks of many who are around and have become "enemies of the cross of Christ." Paul says "their god is their stomach," which means they live for themselves. Paul also says "their glory is in their shame."

Many times we are going to cry for people who are put there by the enemy to make us give up and leave everything. But I have good news for you: Jesus fights for you and backs you up! Paul says these types of people's "destiny is destruction," eternal fire! Could this be the reason Paul is crying? Could it be because of the anguish of seeing them headed to hell even though they know the gospel? Paul's reaction toward these people is immense sadness. God's sadness is much more! Unfortunately there are people like that in our churches, and as Paul says, many of them. Our responsibility is to pray for them, not to persecute them; to love and discipline them.

Returning to the parable of the weed, we should consider that the enemy sowed weeds while the workers were sleeping. What is the secret, then? For the church to be in prayer and in constant dependence on God. In this way the church will have the capacity to love even those who have caused pain to the body of Christ, knowing it belongs to God. Christ is the one who suffers the most in these situations. Doesn't a father suffer when his child takes the wrong steps and causes harm to others?

Scriptural Context

Watch out for false prophets. They come to you in sheep's clothing, but inwardly they are ferocious wolves. By their fruit you will recognize them. Do people pick grapes from thornbushes, or figs from thistles? Likewise, every good tree bears good fruit, but a bad tree bears bad fruit. (Matthew 7:15–17)

These people are grumblers and faultfinders; they follow their own evil desires; they boast about themselves and flatter others for their own advantage. (Jude 1:16)

But the cowardly, the unbelieving, the vile, the murderers, the sexually immoral, those who practice magic arts, the idolaters and all liars—they will be consigned to the fiery lake of burning sulfur. This is the second death. (Revelation 21:8)

For Further Study
2 Peter 2:10–19

Journal

I invite you, in a very personal way, to think about people like the ones who are described in this passage. Pray for them. Ask God for forgiveness for them. Pray for their salvation.

_____

_____

_____

_____

_____

_____

_____

_____

_____

_____

_____

_____

_____

_____

_____

_____

_____

_____

_____

_____

_____

_____

_____

_____

_____

_____

_____

_____

_____

_____

_____

PRAYER

Lord, open our eyes to be able to see the hungry wolves dressed as
lambs. Help us pray for them and show them that there is abundant
life and salvation for them. Father, let us be humble, loving others as
ourselves.

UNIT 4
HEALTHY COUNSEL

65
PAUL'S PRIDE, HIS DISCIPLES

SCRIPTURE
Philippians 4:1

DEVOTIONAL REFLECTION
Immediately, Paul talks to the church in Philippi with affectionate terms: "my brothers and sisters, you whom I love and long for, my joy and crown . . . dear friends!" These expressions are not just empty compliments; they are the result of the sweetness of Jesus in Paul.

Immediately after Paul's compliments of sweetness that flow from his heart, he offers some advice: Stand firm in the Lord. This passage makes us be attentive and merciful toward those brothers and sisters who have fallen because of sin. In the letter to the Ephesians, Paul defines firmness as "being rooted and established in love." Paul's desire is for the church to be unmovable in the Lord and in his love.

SCRIPTURAL CONTEXT
But whoever drinks the water I give them will never thirst. Indeed, the water I give them will become in them a spring of water welling up to eternal life. (John 4:14)

Whoever believes in me, as Scripture has said, rivers of living water will flow from within them. (John 7:38)

I have told you this so that my joy may be in you and that your joy may be complete. (John 15:11)

So, if you think you are standing firm, be careful that you don't fall! (1 Corinthians 10:12)

As you have understood us in part, you will come to understand fully that you can boast of us just as we will boast of you in the day of the Lord Jesus. (2 Corinthians 1:14)

Can both fresh water and salt water flow from the same spring? (James 3:11)

For Further Study
1 Thessalonians 2:19–20
Jude 1:24–25

JOURNAL
Write down, in a sweet way, compliments for your disciples by name.

_____

_____

_____

_____

_____

_____

_____

_____

_____

_____

_____

PRAYER
Lord, prosper us in love! Fill us until we overflow with your love to give it out to a world that desperately seeks love; real love, unconditional love, love that suffers, your love. Help us pour our lives of love out to others, to present your love through our attitudes, our actions, our words, and our deeds. Open our eyes to see the needs of others, and allow us to love them with your love.

66
FIGHTING BETWEEN CHRISTIANS

SCRIPTURE
Philippians 4:2–3

DEVOTIONAL REFLECTION
Paul begins these verses with a strong petition: "I plead." This shows that he is strict and loving at the same time. There is a serious problem among dedicated Christians. These two women are not in agreement; in other words, they are not having the mindset of Christ; they are in disagreement with each other about Jesus's purpose for the church.

Paul is strong in his appeal because of the consequences of the problem, not only because of the disagreement between these women but because their disagreement is in opposition to the purpose of God for the church. Paul does not leave the matter in the air. He takes intentional measures to solve the problem by asking others in the church of Philippi—specifically one person, his "true companion," to help these women come to an agreement.

An ethical person is a transparent person, and his words are always sincere. In these times, even in the churches, there are people who express themselves in one way when they are in front of the crowd and in a completely different way when they are somewhere else. Be aware that eloquence is not equivalent to holiness.

SCRIPTURAL CONTEXT
How good and pleasant it is when God's people live together in unity!
(Psalm 133:1)

Live in harmony with one another. Do not be proud, but be willing to associate with people of low position. Do not be conceited. Do not repay anyone evil for evil. Be careful to do what is right in the eyes of everyone.

If it is possible, as far as it depends on you, live at peace with everyone. (Romans 12:16-18)

I appeal to you, brothers and sisters, in the name of our Lord Jesus Christ, that all of you agree with one another in what you say and that there be no divisions among you, but that you be perfectly united in mind and thought. (1 Corinthians 1:10)

Make every effort to live in peace with everyone and to be holy; without holiness no one will see the Lord. (Hebrews 12:14)

For Further Study
Mark 9:50
James 3:14–16

JOURNAL

Seeing the way Paul deals with the problem between two sisters fighting in church, how would you deal with a similar problem between two people in your own church?

_____

_____

_____

_____

_____

_____

_____

_____

_____

_____

_____

_____

_____

_____

_____

_____

_____

_____

_____

_____

_____

_____

_____

_____

_____

_____

_____

_____

_____

_____

_____

_____

_____

_____

_____

PRAYER

Lord, as believers, we are your representatives. Help us always be in Christ and not allow our personal agendas to compromise your purpose for the church. We want to always remember that we are not part of an enterprise; we are part of the body of Christ, which is your church.

67 ᔔ
INCREDIBLE ADVICE

SCRIPTURE
Philippians 4:2–4

DEVOTIONAL REFLECTION

Paul gives a second piece of advice to the church in Philippi. First he asks the sisters (Euodia and Syntyche) who are fighting to be of the same mind even though they disagree on various issues. He pleads for them to think like Christ, to have the mind of Christ. Then he invites them to live in the joy of the Lord. He invites them to consider all the time that they are in Christ. Paul is emphatic in this second piece of advice or admonition; he even repeats it: "I will say it again: Rejoice!"

It is curious that, after the disagreement between two sisters, the next advice is to rejoice. Do not allow any situation, no matter how hard it is, make you lose the joy of God. Once again, Paul says that the key of any aspect of the Christian life is to be found in Christ.

Joy is part of the fruit of the Spirit. Joy is the result of knowing we have a future hope. Even though we are sentimental and emotional beings, I think we will never stop being so, for it is part of our human nature. Joy transcends feelings and emotions, even though they are also part of joy.

Paul's order to rejoice is an invitation to bring light, happiness, hope, and motivation wherever we find ourselves, whether in good or bad situations. It is an invitation to spread the fruit of the Holy Spirit to others.

SCRIPTURAL CONTEXT

I will extol the LORD at all times; his praise will always be on my lips. I will glory in the LORD; let the afflicted hear and rejoice. Glorify the LORD with me; let us exalt his name together. (Psalm 34:1–3)

Rejoice and be glad, because great is your reward in heaven, for in the same way they persecuted the prophets who were before you. (Matthew 5:12)

I have told you this so that my joy may be in you and that your joy may be complete. (John 15:11)

Be joyful in hope, patient in affliction, faithful in prayer. (Romans 12:12)

For Further Study
Psalm 34:1–3
Galatians 5:22–23
Isaiah 61:10–11

JOURNAL

Have you lost the joy of God because of disagreements with other people? How can you recover that joy? Write your thoughts in the following lines.

_____

_____

_____

_____

_____

_____

_____

_____

_____

_____

PRAYER

Lord, may your joy flow through my life, my conversation, my attitudes, and in the midst of any situation.

68 ❧
HOW DO MY LOVED ONES KNOW ME?

SCRIPTURE

Philippians 4:5

Let your forbearance be known unto all men. The Lord is at hand. (ASV)

Let everyone see that you are considerate in all you do. Remember, the Lord is coming soon. (NLT)

Make it as clear as you can to all you meet that you're on their side, working with them and not against them. Help them see that the Master is about to arrive. He could show up any minute! (MSG)

DEVOTIONAL REFLECTION

Philippians 4:5 is the third piece of advice from Paul to the Philippians. The first is not to fight but to have the mind of Christ, to be of the same mind; the second is to rejoice in the Lord always. Now he invites them to control their own tempers.

We are all different. Some are passive, others are almost electric, others are reflective. But we should all be holy, and that is why we should surrender our character to the sovereignty of God. Even though we are different, we are part of one body, and we should live according to that. Paul invites us to be gentle, kind, and good. He asks us to let that mark us (see the different versions of Philippians 4:5 above).

Once more, the key is found in Philippians 3:9 "to be found in him." As we are submerged and are in him, unity, joy, and gentleness are produced from the inside out. Jesus is one with the Father and with the Holy Spirit: Only in him is there unity. The fruit of the Spirit is joy; only in him is there joy. Only in him is there kindness, humility, gentleness, and goodness. Really, in Christ is the key.

Scriptural Context

You have heard that it was said, "Eye for eye, and tooth for tooth." But I tell you, do not resist an evil person. If anyone slaps you on the right cheek, turn to them the other cheek also. And if anyone wants to sue you and take your shirt, hand over your coat as well. If anyone forces you to go one mile, go with them two miles. Give to the one who asks you, and do not turn away from the one who wants to borrow from you. You have heard that it was said, "Love your neighbor and hate your enemy." But I tell you, love your enemies and pray for those who persecute you, that you may be children of your Father in heaven. He causes his sun to rise on the evil and the good, and sends rain on the righteous and the unrighteous. (Matthew 5:38–45)

For Further Study
Matthew 11:29–30
1 Corinthians 9:25–27

Journal

Reply to the following questions based on the text and the scriptures found in the Scriptural Context section. What is the cause, and what is the effect? Is unity that produces joy or joy that produces unity? Is it gentleness or kindness that produce joy or unity? Or what?

_____

_____

_____

_____

_____

_____

_____

_____

_____

_____

_____

_____

_____

_____

_____

_____

_____

_____

_____

_____

_____

_____

_____

_____

_____

_____

_____

_____

_____

PRAYER

Lord, help us to let you shine in us, through us, and toward others.
Help us to reflect only you. Do what is necessary in order for us to
surrender and let you be the one who responds through us in every
circumstance of our lives. Give us the awareness that you are near!

69 ❧
LORD, TEACH US TO PRAY

SCRIPTURE
Philippians 4:6

DEVOTIONAL REFLECTION

"Do not be anxious about anything" is one of the Bible's pieces of advice that is the hardest to accept. Preoccupation comes from uncertainty of the future, from the consequences of our actions and decisions, and from the unexpected surprises of life. We really do not have control of the future, nor of the surprises that might unexpectedly come in life. We have control of our decisions and actions, but we do not have control of the consequences they will produce. What should we do then?

Paul's answer to that question is quite clear. We should present our requests to God. There are times that we knock on every door and talk to a lot of people to get something we need. Then we finally come to God in prayer as our last resource. Paul is practical in everything: First he invites us to pray about things out of our control, for what gives us anxiety, and for the consequences of our well-intentioned and ethical decisions. The answer to anxiety, worry, or preoccupation is to trust God in prayer.

There are two parts in the request—prayer and petition. The first has to do with communication; the second has to do with intensity. The truth is that God knows our needs, our worries, and our desires. As we pray we consciously declare that he already knows our needs, but we also express our trust in him, and we declare it seriously and with intensity.

The last part is to recognize that he has heard us, telling him that we accept his answer, whatever it may be, with thanksgiving.

For God everything is possible. Remember that God has the last word in everything.

SCRIPTURAL CONTEXT

Therefore I tell you, do not worry about your life, what you will eat or drink; or about your body, what you will wear. Is not life more than food, and the body more than clothes? (Matthew 6:25)

And pray in the Spirit on all occasions with all kinds of prayers and requests. With this in mind, be alert and always keep on praying for all the Lord's people. (Ephesians 6:18)

Pray continually, give thanks in all circumstances; for this is God's will for you in Christ Jesus. (1 Thessalonians 5:17–18)

When you ask, you do not receive, because you ask with wrong motives, that you may spend what you get on your pleasures. You adulterous people, don't you know that friendship with the world means enmity against God? Therefore, anyone who chooses to be a friend of the world becomes an enemy of God. (James 4:3–4)

For Further Study
Matthew 6:5–15
Luke 11:1–12
1 Timothy 2:1–4

JOURNAL

How do you proceed when you go through a difficult situation? Give your answer based on the text and on the passages in the Scriptural Context section.

_____

_____

_____

_____

_____

_____

_____

_____

_____

_____

_____

_____

_____

_____

_____

_____

_____

_____

_____

_____

_____

PRAYER

Lord, teach us how to pray.

70 &

CAPTIVE IN CHRIST

SCRIPTURE
Philippians 4:7–9

DEVOTIONAL REFLECTION
Paul continues to give advice to the Philippians. Now he talks about something that every believer should practice. Paul's interest is for the believer to have a healthy mind. What comes into our minds is processed by our hearts, and the heart expresses itself out loud through our words. The advice is wise and practical. This is one of the most important disciplines for spiritual, mental, and physical health. A person throws garbage to his mind through what he thinks, sees, and reads, and this ends up contaminating his heart, his vocabulary, and, consequently, all the people around him. He becomes a negative person, a bitter root (see Hebrews 12:15). Soon, feeding ourselves with negativity begins to bear negative fruit, and the effect is pollution of our personality, home, friendships, and everything around us.

Paul concludes his advice by saying that what he advises the Philippians to do is what he already practices. In other words, he's not being a hypocrite. He's practicing what he's preaching. The result of the practice of putting our thoughts captive in Christ is peace and nothing more and nothing less than the presence of God. What an encouragement, what a great support, knowing that when we learn to govern our thoughts, we guarantee the presence of God in our lives, in those around our home, in our community, in our congregation! The health of our mind is an agent of change.

SCRIPTURAL CONTEXT

In his pride the wicked man does not seek him; in all his thoughts there is no room for God. (Psalm 10:4)

You brood of vipers, how can you who are evil say anything good? For the mouth speaks what the heart is full of. A good man brings good things out of the good stored up in him, and an evil man brings evil things out of the evil stored up in him. (Matthew 12:34–35)

Love must be sincere. Hate what is evil; cling to what is good. (Romans 12:9)

We demolish arguments and every pretension that sets itself up against the knowledge of God, and we take captive every thought to make it obedient to Christ. (2 Corinthians 10:5)

For Further Study
Ephesians 4:25
Ephesians 5:8–10
2 Corinthians 13:7–8

JOURNAL

Make a list of how you can transform your mind according to what Paul advises. Mention some concrete examples of things you should avoid and things you should put into practice.

_____

_____

_____

_____

_____

_____

_____

_____

_____

_____

_____

_____

_____

_____

_____

_____

_____

_____

_____

_____

_____

_____

_____

_____

_____

_____

_____

_____

_____

PRAYER

Lord, take our minds and direct them toward whatever is true, whatever is noble, whatever is pure, whatever is lovely, whatever is admirable, whatever is excellent or praiseworthy.

71 ✀
PEACE

SCRIPTURE
Philippians 4:7, 9

DEVOTIONAL REFLECTION
In verse 7, Paul starts by saying: "And the peace of God." The peace of God is God's gift to everyone who seeks unity, who lives in the joy of the Lord, who is good, and who has full trust in God. Truly, it is a peace that transcends all understanding. The peace of God (or complete health, complete integrity, absence of contradiction) is something that cannot be rationalized or understood. It is supernatural! It is a miracle!

There is only one place of protection in the whole universe, and that is in Christ Jesus. God is a God of peace who assures his presence to his people when they are willing to live in Christ. There is no safer place than to be in the presence of God! Dwelling in him assures us peace and joy. The peace of God protects us from ourselves; it guards our hearts and our minds.

SCRIPTURAL CONTEXT
You will keep in perfect peace those whose minds are steadfast, because they trust in you. Trust in the LORD forever, for the LORD, the LORD himself, is the Rock eternal. (Isaiah 26:3-4)

Peace I leave with you; my peace I give you. I do not give to you as the world gives. Do not let your hearts be troubled and do not be afraid. (John 14:27)

The weapons we fight with are not the weapons of the world. On the contrary, they have divine power to demolish strongholds. (2 Corinthians 10:4)

Let the peace of Christ rule in your hearts, since as members of one body you were called to peace. And be thankful. (Colossians 3:15)

For Further Study
Matthew 15:19–20
Philippians 4:8
1 Peter 1:5

JOURNAL

Write the benefits of being in the presence of God, in Christ.

_____

_____

_____

_____

_____

_____

_____

_____

_____

_____

_____

_____

_____

_____

PRAYER

"Peace, peace, wonderful peace! Peace, peace, glorious peace! Since my Redeemer has ransomed my soul I have peace, sweet peace." (*Sing to the Lord* #418)

72 ～
CONTENTMENT

SCRIPTURE
Philippians 4:10–12

DEVOTIONAL REFLECTION

In these verses, Paul presents his philosophy of life regarding prosperity. He is sure God will never leave him. However, he did not come up with this philosophy suddenly. He acquired his conviction progressively: "for I have *learned*." It is a learning experience; it is the result of practicing the presence of God in his life.

Paul is not deceived by a worldly prosperity. His goal was never to be prosperous. His goal is to be found in Christ. He experiences many pleasant situations as well as difficult ones. Our needs should not prevent us from living a life in God. Paul knows how to live in him!

There will always be someone there to take us by the hand, as long as we remain in Christ. The key to Paul's learning experience is that he has learned to be content. His satisfaction is not based on what is temporary but on what is eternal.

This is not a calling to poverty. If God asks that of anyone, he should respond accordingly. It is not a calling to hoarding, or to excessive acquisitions. It is a calling to contentment, to know that in Jesus we are safe in spite of the conditions, for we are 100 percent fulfilling his will.

SCRIPTURAL CONTEXT

So do not worry, saying, 'What shall we eat?' or 'What shall we drink?' or 'What shall we wear?' For the pagans run after all these things, and your heavenly Father knows that you need them. But seek first his kingdom and his righteousness, and all these things will be given to you as well. Therefore do not worry about tomorrow, for tomorrow will worry about itself. Each day has enough trouble of its own. (Matthew 6:31–34)

For you know the grace of our Lord Jesus Christ, that though he was rich, yet for your sake he became poor, so that you through his poverty might become rich. (2 Corinthians 8:9)

I have labored and toiled and have often gone without sleep; I have known hunger and thirst and have often gone without food; I have been cold and naked. (2 Corinthians 11:27)

For Further Study
2 Corinthians 7:6–7
2 Corinthians 11:9
Galatians 6:10

JOURNAL

How can you be content when you are facing difficult situations? Write down some practical actions that you can learn and put into practice in order to depend on God for everything.

_____

_____

_____

_____

_____

_____

_____

_____

_____

PRAYER

Lord, let us know when we are not seeking your kingdom and righteousness. Help us seek you, and know that in you, we will have what is necessary in order to fulfill your will, and above all, let us be the type of people who are willing to extend a hand to those who need it.

73

I AM NOT SUPERMAN

SCRIPTURE
Philippians 4:13

DEVOTIONAL REFLECTION
"I can do all this" refers to the hardships we face as the kingdom of God advances in our surroundings. For Paul, it means the difficulties he faces while he's stuck in prison. It does *not* refer to being Superman, or to achieving dreams and goals that are not in the will of God. It does not mean I leave a situation in God's hands and then run out to solve everything without allowing God to work. In Christ (see Philippians 3:9) is the condition, state, way of life in which Paul can do all this—"this" being his achievement of contentment and peace in God even while in prison. The key is to abide in Jesus.

"I can do all this" is only for believers, for disciples; it is not a promise to attract the crowds or to make ourselves famous. It is a promise for those who want to risk it all to live in Christ and to know the power of his resurrection (Philippians 3:10). It is Christ who strengthens. It is not about our own efforts, our devotions, our prayers, or our fasting (even though these disciplines are important for the development of the Christian character). There is nothing safer than to affirm ourselves in the Rock that is God to remain safe in such a changing world. It is really crazy to live without Christ and outside the will and purpose of God for our lives.

SCRIPTURAL CONTEXT

Remain in me, as I also remain in you. No branch can bear fruit by itself; it must remain in the vine. Neither can you bear fruit unless you remain in me. "I am the vine; you are the branches. If you remain in me and I in you, you will bear much fruit; apart from me you can do nothing. (John 15:4–5)

Such confidence we have through Christ before God. Not that we are competent in ourselves to claim anything for ourselves, but our competence comes from God. (2 Corinthians 3:4–5)

I pray that out of his glorious riches he may strengthen you with power through his Spirit in your inner being. (Ephesians 3:16)

Finally, be strong in the Lord and in his mighty power. (Ephesians 6:10)

For Further Study
Psalm 18:1–2
Psalm 46:1–5
Isaiah 40:29–31
2 Corinthians 12:9–10
Colossians 1:11–12

JOURNAL

It there anything that causes you insecurity? Where do you find your strength? What does "I can do all things" mean for Paul and for you?

_____

_____

_____

_____

_____

_____

_____

_____

_____

_____

_____

_____

_____

_____

_____

_____

_____

_____

_____

_____

_____

_____

_____

_____

_____

_____

_____

_____

_____

_____

_____

PRAYER

Lord, thank you for the power of your resurrection in our lives.
Thank you for your strength and for being the power of God in us for
all the situations we face daily as we present ourselves to you with our
whole being.

74

TAKING CARE OF OUR PASTORS

SCRIPTURE
Philippians 4:14–16

DEVOTIONAL REFLECTION
Paul did not arrive in Philippi out of his own initiative or out of a personal strategy. He was there because of God's vision and the direction of the Holy Spirit (see Acts 16). When God leads us to a place, we can trust that when we go through problems, he is there to back us up and guide us to all truth.

Philippi is the first church in Europe. The first convert there is Lydia, a woman who has a lot of resources. Then some other Jewish women follow. The second group of converts is the prison guard and his family. It is a church made up of different social classes, but it is a generous church. This is the church that sustains Paul for the most part in his mission of taking the gospel to the Gentiles. They never forget their missionary pastor. They accompany him and never stop sustaining him economically.

Paul expresses that he had "needs." However, he is mentioning it when he has already received help to cover them. Paul does not ask help from the churches for his needs. He is not a burden for anyone. He receives help because of the love of the believers. We have to be attentive to the needs of our brothers and sisters before we are asked for help; we should be moved by love. Paul trusts in the Lord, that he has given him the vision and sent him (see Acts 26:17–18).

As pastors, we should be careful not to ask for so much help for our needs, and much less for our desires. Paul is very clear in his philosophy of life in order to keep his vision and mission (see Philippians 4:11–13). A church that takes care of its pastors is a church that is blessed by God.

Scriptural Context

And when I was with you and needed something, I was not a burden to anyone, for the brothers who came from Macedonia supplied what I needed. I have kept myself from being a burden to you in any way, and will continue to do so. (2 Corinthians 11:9)

Remember your leaders, who spoke the word of God to you. Consider the outcome of their way of life and imitate their faith. (Hebrews 13:7)

When you ask, you do not receive, because you ask with wrong motives, that you may spend what you get on your pleasures. You adulterous people, don't you know that friendship with the world means enmity against God? (James 4:3-4a)

Now we ask you, brothers and sisters, to acknowledge those who work hard among you, who care for you in the Lord and who admonish you. Hold them in the highest regard in love because of their work. Live in peace with each other. (1 Thessalonians 5:12–13)

For Further Study
Matthew 25:21
Philippians 1:7

Journal

Do you take care of those who have guided you in the way of God? What can you do for them? In what ways can we inspire others through our faith? Write about it in the following lines.

_____

_____

_____

_____

_____

_____

_____

_____

_____

_____

_____

_____

_____

_____

_____

_____

_____

_____

_____

_____

_____

_____

_____

_____

_____

_____

PRAYER

Lord, help us remember our pastors and missionaries. Help us take care of them and be more generous with them, knowing you have sent them to feed and seek the lost ones. But above all, may your hand of power sustain them when they go through difficult circumstances and are far away from their families.

75

THE RESULTS OF GENEROSITY

SCRIPTURE
Philippians 4:18–20

And my God shall supply every need of yours according to his riches in glory in Christ Jesus. (Philippians 4:19, ASV)

You can be sure that God will take care of everything you need, his generosity exceeding even yours in the glory that pours from Jesus. (Philippians 4:19, MSG)

And this same God who takes care of me will supply all your needs from his glorious riches, which have been given to us in Christ Jesus. (Philippians 4:19, NLT)

DEVOTIONAL REFLECTION
Verse 19 is a classic. The source of "the riches of his glory" is Christ Jesus. Jesus is the most precious treasure, the pearl of great value. Jesus is our everything, and he meets our needs, whether physical, emotional, or material. Jesus uses his church to meet the needs of his own. Whatever we give as a church or as believers becomes "a fragrant offering, an acceptable sacrifice, pleasing to God." In the midst of these words there is a secret: We should give with sacrifice, not from our leftovers. This applies both to those who have a lot as well as to those who have little.

The final result is double: 1) the essential needs of our brothers and sisters are met, as well as those of people who are not yet Christians but are in need; 2) ultimately, our God and Father receives all the glory for ever and ever.

When we give to others, we receive. Many times, I imagine some people will get to heaven, and Jesus will say, "I had so much to give you, but you didn't receive it."

Then they will answer, "Why didn't you give it to me, Lord?"

And he will reply, "Because you didn't obey in giving to others, and your hands were busy treasuring the little you had, which prevented you from receiving the rest."

SCRIPTURAL CONTEXT

For the LORD God is a sun and shield; the LORD bestows favor and honor; no good thing does he withhold from those whose walk is blameless. LORD Almighty, blessed is the one who trusts in you. (Psalms 84:11–12)

But as for me, I watch in hope for the LORD, I wait for God my Savior; my God will hear me. (Micah 7:7)

Praise be to the God and Father of our Lord Jesus Christ, who has blessed us in the heavenly realms with every spiritual blessing in Christ. (Ephesians 1:3)

His divine power has given us everything we need for a godly life through our knowledge of him who called us by his own glory and goodness. (2 Peter 1:3)

It is because of him that you are in Christ Jesus, who has become for us wisdom from God—that is, our righteousness, holiness and redemption. (1 Corinthians 1:30)

For Further Study
Genesis 48:15
Psalm 23:1–5
Romans 9:23
Romans 11:33–36

JOURNAL

Write about how God takes care of you today and give him thanks.

_____

_____

_____

_____

_____

_____

_____

_____

_____

_____

_____

_____

_____

_____

_____

_____

_____

_____

PRAYER

Lord, move us as a church to be generous to meet all the needs around us. May the purpose not be to receive praise but for you to be able to manifest yourself through us, "the aroma of the knowledge of him everywhere," and may we be "to God the pleasing aroma of Christ among those who are being saved and those who are perishing" (2 Corinthians 2:14–15). Amen.

76 ❦
HOLY PEOPLE WHO HUG

SCRIPTURE
Philippians 4:21–22

DEVOTIONAL REFLECTION
The main characteristic of the members of a church is God's people in Christ Jesus. God's people in Christ Jesus are the people who are submerged, soaked, saturated in Jesus Christ. They are the saints—that is, they are separated, set apart, and exclusive to impregnate their surroundings with Christ Jesus, showing him to their loved ones and anyone who is in contact with them. "Saints in Christ Jesus" is a phrase that denotes the purpose and mission of the church. The purpose is that they are set apart for the mission.

In fact, even in terrible circumstances, such as the deplorable conditions of a prison in Rome, Paul, who is in Christ, sends greetings from the prison guards there. Paul has established a church among the guards (see Philippians 1:12–14). Being in prison is not a waste of time. The purpose of Paul's life and the mission of Christ to make disciples is carried on. The enemy is clever in making us waste time. But in Paul's case, not even prison stops the progress of the gospel.

"Greet" and "send you greetings" are interesting expressions. The original is a compound word. The first part of the word means to unite or tighten. The second part means to hug. That is, a greeting is unity through a hug. The brothers and sisters in Philippi and the brothers and sisters in Rome are tightly united by a hug.

The central theme of the letter is unity (see Philippians 2:5). The central theme is to think like Christ, have the attitude of Christ, be in Christ. "Greet . . . send you greetings" is the hug of God's people in Christ Jesus to God's people in the house of Caesar. The house of Caesar, a corrupt and cruel human structure, now has saints in Christ

Jesus. A holy hug is more effective than the most eloquent of sermons, and even more so for those who are facing difficult situations.

SCRIPTURAL CONTEXT

You are the salt of the earth. But if the salt loses its saltiness, how can it be made salty again? It is no longer good for anything, except to be thrown out and trampled underfoot. You are the light of the world. A town built on a hill cannot be hidden. (Matthew 5:13–14)

Greet one another with a holy kiss. All the churches of Christ send greetings. (Romans 16:16)

Paul and Timothy, servants of Christ Jesus, to all God's holy people in Christ Jesus at Philippi, together with the overseers and deacons. (Philippians 1:1)

To the church of God in Corinth, to those sanctified in Christ Jesus and called to be his holy people, together with all those everywhere who call on the name of our Lord Jesus Christ—their Lord and ours. (1 Corinthians 1:2)

JOURNAL

Write down your thoughts about God's people who hug each other. How does this relate to the mission of the church? How does this relate to the theme of the letter to the Philippians?

_____

_____

_____

_____

_____

_____

_____

_____

_____

_____

_____

_____

_____

_____

_____

_____

_____

_____

_____

_____

_____

_____

_____

_____

_____

_____

_____

_____

_____

_____

PRAYER

Lord, thank you for the great example of the apostle Paul. He motivates us to open homes to transform our corrupt society, which is lost and without hope, with the best of messages, in Christ Jesus. Help us to hug in Christ those who need it so much.

77 ❧
THANK YOU FOR YOUR GRACE!

SCRIPTURE
Philippians 4:23

DEVOTIONAL REFLECTION
Paul finishes his letter by mentioning an attribute of Jesus Christ—grace. Jesus, by his own will and because of love for us, poured his life freely and by grace as a sacrifice for me, to save me and give me life abundant. His grace is so amazing, sublime, splendid, marvelous, and loving! Jesus is unbelievable, and the grace he gives us is amazing.

Paul offers a similar farewell in his second letter to the Corinthians, where he shows the sequence of the triune God (see 2 Corinthians 13:14). God's love invites his church to unite, by grace, with Jesus in holy communion. Paul not only presents Jesus as the Lord of grace, but he also desires the same grace for the brothers and sisters.

It is all only because of the grace of God, not because we deserve it, nor because we have a certain last name or hierarchical position. Forgetting the grace of God makes us miss the target.

SCRIPTURAL CONTEXT
But the angel said to her, "Do not be afraid, Mary; you have found favor with God. You will conceive and give birth to a son, and you are to call him Jesus." (Luke 1:30–31)

And the child grew and became strong; he was filled with wisdom, and the grace of God was on him. (Luke 2:40)

The God of peace will soon crush Satan under your feet. The grace of our Lord Jesus be with you. (Romans 16:20)

But by the grace of God I am what I am, and his grace to me was not without effect. No, I worked harder than all of them—yet not I, but the grace of God that was with me. (1 Corinthians 15:10)

May the grace of the Lord Jesus Christ, and the love of God, and the fellowship of the Holy Spirit be with you all. (2 Corinthians 13:14)

JOURNAL

What has the grace of God meant for you in light of reading the letter to the Philippians?

_____

_____

_____

_____

_____

_____

_____

_____

_____

_____

_____

_____

_____

_____

_____

_____

PRAYER

Lord, your love is so great that it cannot be calculated or measured. And that love was expressed by Jesus in grace; grace that transforms and that is not in vain. It is worth repeating: Thank you for your grace!